D0218447

LESLIE HIGH SCHOOL LIBRARY

Historic Highway Bridges of Michigan

Historic Highway Bridges of Michigan

CHARLES K. HYDE

Charles K. Hyde

9/16/1995

 Wayne State University Press Detroit

GREAT LAKES BOOKS

*A complete listing of the books in this series
can be found at the back of this volume.*

Philip P. Mason, *Editor*
Department of History, Wayne State University

Dr. Charles K. Hyde, *Associate Editor*
Department of History, Wayne State University

Copyright © 1993 by Wayne State University Press,
Detroit, Michigan 48202. All rights are reserved.
No part of this book may be reproduced without formal permission.
Manufactured in the United States of America.

99 98 97 96 95 94 93   5 4 3 2 1

Library of Congress Cataloging–in–Publication Data
Hyde, Charles K., 1945–
    Historic highway bridges of Michigan / Charles K. Hyde.
    p.   cm.   —(Great Lakes Books)
    Includes bibliographical references and index.
    ISBN 0–8143–2448–7 (pbk. : alk. paper)
    1. Historic bridges—Michigan.. 2. Bridges—Michigan—Design and
construction—History. I Title. II. Series.
    TG24.M45H93 1993
    624'.2'09774—dc20   92–37712

Cover photo: Leonard Street bridge (1879) over the
Grand River, Grand Rapids. Courtesy of the State
Archives of Michigan.

Back cover photos: Upper left hand corner is the
Mortimer E. Cooley Bridge (1934) over the Pine
River, Manistee County. Photo courtesy of MDOT.
Lower right hand corner is a bowstring arch bridge,
assembled in downtown Owosso, Shiawassee County,
January, 1895. Courtesy of the State Archives of
Michigan.

Title page photo spread: Insterstate 75 (Mackinac Straits)
Bridge. Courtesy of MDOT.

Special Acknowledgment: Grateful acknowledgment is
made to the Mackinac Bridge Authority for financial
assistance in the publication of this volume.

Contents

Foreword:
Historic Bridge Preservation—Problems
and Prospects *by Paul McAllister*   7

Acknowledgments   15

Introduction   17

Chapter **1** *Michigan's Transportation*
Systems in the Nineteenth and Twentieth
Centuries: From Wagon Paths
to Superhighways   19

Highway Bridge Construction:
Politics and Economics   23

The Twentieth Century:
The Automobile Age   31

The Structure and Financing of
Highway Improvements   33

Highway Bridge Construction
Comes of Age   35

Chapter **2** *American Bridge Designs*
of the Nineteenth Century and Their
Michigan Reflections   47

Masonry Arch Bridges   50
Timber Truss Bridges   53
Metal Truss Bridges   59
   Miscellaneous Through Trusses   64
   Pratt Through Trusses   73
   Warren Through Trusses   77
   Miscellaneous Pony Trusses   79
   Pratt Pony Trusses   82
   Warren Pony Trusses   84
   Deck Trusses   85

Chapter **3** *American Bridge Designs*
of the Twentieth Century and Their
Michigan Reflections   89

Steel Girder Bridges   89

Moveable Bridges   92

   Swing Bridges   93

   Bascule Bridges   99

   Vertical Lift Bridges   101

Other Steel Bridges   102

   Steel Arches   102

   Cantilevered Steel Trusses   106

   Steel Suspension   109

Reinforced Concrete Bridges   112

   Earth-Filled Concrete Arches   117

   Open Spandrel Concrete Arches   123

   Through Concrete Arches   127

   Concrete Girders   131

   Concrete Camelbacks   135

Chapter **4** *Bridge Design and*
Construction in Michigan Since
World War II   143

Chapter **5** *Michigan's Big Bridges,*
From Ambassador to Zilwaukee   147

Ambassador Bridge   147

Blue Water Bridge   152

Houghton-Hancock Bridge   152

International Bridge   159

Mackinac Straits Bridge   159

Zilwaukee Bridge   166

Appendix **A** *Regional Maps*
Showing Bridge Locations   169

Appendix **B** *Builders of Michigan's*
Metal Truss Bridges   179

Bibliography   183

Index   187

Foreword

Historic Bridge Preservation— Problems and Prospects

by Paul McAllister

Bureau of Transportation Planning, Michigan Department of Transportation

Michigan's historic highway bridges are rapidly disappearing. State and local governments are tearing them down and replacing them because they are deteriorating, or are too narrow or too weak to carry present-day loads safely. Of the 140 bridges originally listed in the historic bridge inventory in 1986 as historically significant, more than half have already disappeared or will be replaced by the turn of the century. Historic highway bridges are truly a declining and endangered species.

It became apparent almost a decade ago that these historic bridges were about to disappear rapidly. Federal legislation regarding the preservation of historically significant properties, especially the National Historic Preservation Act (1966), came into play when states used federal funds for bridge replacement. Critical bridge funding came with the requirement that government units replacing bridges must review them for their historic and engineering significance. This gave preservationists, especially State Historic Preservation Officers (SHPOs), a legal voice in decisions regarding the demolition of historic bridges. The SHPO for the state of Michigan therefore became directly involved in determining the historical significance of Michigan's highway bridges.

Federal laws protecting historic resources are stringent, and complying with them requires rigorous documentation and justification. To be considered a significant historic resource and therefore protected by these federal laws, the resource—whether building, structure, or archaeological site— must be listed or determined eligible for listing on the National Register of Historic Places, a program administered by the National Park Service, United States Department of the Interior. In Michigan, the Bureau of History (BOH), Michigan Department of State, administers the program under the auspices of the State Historic Preservation Office.

To be listed on the National Register, the resource must meet certain standards of significance, and for privately owned properties, the owner must approve the listing. A resource, however, also may be determined eligible for listing on the National Register and still be protected by federal law. The Keeper of the National Register makes that determination after the state or federal agency concerned with the resource submits information. Publicly owned structures, however, may be listed on the National Register without the owner's consent.

For transportation projects, two primary pieces of federal legislation protect significant historic resources including bridges: the National Historic Preservation Act and the Department of Transportation Act. The Historic Preservation Act requires consultation between the transportation agencies proposing to carry out the project affecting the historic bridge and the historic preservation agencies charged with protecting historic resources. Although the consultation process is not binding, it requires a thorough review of all options and is intended to lead to an

agreement on the least destructive yet practical option. The Transportation Act is more stringent: it requires that the agency proposing an action causing an adverse or damaging effect on a historic resource must show that there is no "prudent and feasible alternative" to the proposed action and that the agency has incorporated "all possible planning to minimize harm" into the proposed project. These two pieces of legislation and their implementing regulations guarantee that any Michigan Department of Transportation (MDOT) project involving historic bridges or other historic sites receives vigorous and thorough review.

Determining these old and rapidly deteriorating bridges to be significant historic structures imposed a whole new set of hurdles in the way of replacing them. As preservationists discovered the history of these bridges, transportation agencies recognized that these structures were rapidly becoming obsolete or unsafe. State transportation offi-

cials clamored for more money to correct this national problem, and the federal government responded with new programs such as the Critical Bridge Fund. At the same time, the government created another major obstacle to replacing these bridges—federal legislation protecting historic resources.

Complying with the often confusing and technically complicated federal regulations protecting these historic bridges has frustrated the people trying to reconcile the need to provide safe bridges with the need to preserve our cultural heritage. The time required to assess each bridge individually frustrated the transportation officials trying to replace these decaying bridges as quickly as possible. Similarly, preservationists felt frustrated because they had to decide which of these old bridges were significant when they knew little about them.

Information on the total numbers of historic bridges of the various types and their distribution throughout the state did not exist, much less detailed information on individual bridges. Moreover, the BOH had neither systematic knowledge of the history of country, state, and federal involvement in bridge building in Michigan, nor information about the persons and firms who designed and built these structures. This lack of information made it impossible to place an individual bridge within a historical context, and decisions about the historic significance of any particular bridge became difficult.

The initial impetus to develop ways to treat bridge preservation in a systematic way came from the Federal Highway Administration, as part of their Highway Bridge Replacement and Rehabilitation Program. In response to public officials', preservationists', and private citizens' increasing awareness of the need to preserve our nation's historic bridges, the Federal Highway Administration fostered the preparation of inventories of historic bridges. In September 1980, Morris C. Reinhardt, director of the Office of

Engineering of the Federal Highway Administration, urged regional federal highway administrators to work with the state departments of transportation, the state historic preservation officers, and historical societies to inventory and rank historic bridges.

To develop a list of historic bridges in Michigan, the SHPO wanted a survey of Michigan's bridges by a qualified and experienced historian familiar with Michigan's engineering and industrial past. While MDOT initially balked at the expense, effort, and time that such a survey required, they soon saw the advantage of determining which of the thousands of the state's bridges were historic. Such a survey would allow them to allocate resources appropriately. Jointly, the Bureau of History and the Michigan Department of Transportation decided to conduct a historic survey of Michigan bridges.

MDOT engaged staff in its Local Services Division, county road commissions,

and city public works departments to collect historical information about these bridges, including the date of construction, the designer of the bridge, and the company that built it. This information, along with a photograph of each bridge, was important in helping determine the historic significance of these bridges. The BOH and MDOT engaged Charles K. Hyde of Wayne State University to research and write a report outlining the history of bridge building in Michigan and containing an analysis of the inventory data and recommendations on the historic significance of the bridges. Hyde completed his report and recommendations in 1985, after Donald C. Jackson and the SHPO reviewed the report.

Hyde's recommendations provided the basis for developing a final list of some 140 historically significant bridges in Michigan. Only a few of these were already listed on the National Register of Historic Places or determined eligible for listing. The Federal

Highway Administration submitted the remaining bridges to the National Register, which determined them eligible for listing in April and June 1986. MDOT now had a list of the significant historic bridges in Michigan. Subsequently, the federal government required all states to make an inventory of their historic bridges with the Surface Transportation and Uniform Relocation Assistance Act of 1987. Michigan had completed its inventory well before Congress enacted this law and was among the first states to do so.

The next step in this process was to develop a long-range preservation plan for these bridges. Over the next several months, the Bureau of History and MDOT worked out a Programmatic Memorandum of Agreement (PMOA) for a procedure to be followed in determining what should be done about a deficient bridge. The plan involved considering a sequence of ranked standard alternative treatments; the most appropriate treatments from a preservation standpoint were considered before other alternatives.

The Advisory Council on Historic Preservation, a federal advisory body that must approve such agreements, refused to do so because the PMOA was not broad enough, given its failure to consider such issues as bridge approach work, bridges within historic districts, and the relationship of the PMOA to other environmental and cultural resource assessments. Nevertheless, MDOT has attempted to follow the major provisions of the PMOA on a voluntary basis. The standard alternative treatments of historic bridges, as outlined in the PMOA, ranked in order from best to worst, are:

1. *Do nothing.* Sometimes it is practical to maintain the bridge. Many of these older bridges are narrow but otherwise serviceable as long as they continue to be maintained. However, this is generally not a practical alternative for bridges on the heavily traveled state trunkline system or those so deteriorated that routine maintenance no longer keeps them serviceable. It is a practical solution only when traffic volumes are low and the bridges are in good condition.

2. *Build on a new location without using the old bridge.* This is an alternative that is practical only under unusual circumstances. First, there must be the opportunity to relocate the bridge; that is, there must be enough land adjacent to the old bridge or where the new bridge is to be built. Second, there must be a rationale to relocate the bridge; that is, an alignment for the roadway that is more desirable, or at least not any worse, than the present bridge alignment must exist. This alternative is costly because not only must a new bridge be built but the old bridge must also be repaired to function safely as a pedestrian and bicycle bridge. The long-term cost of maintaining the old bridge likewise must be considered, but when we subtract the cost of demolishing the historic

bridge and the permanent loss of this resource, the cost is not great.

The Michigan Department of Transportation has already successfully used this alternative. The department preserved the US-12 bridge in Mottville and the M-26 bridge in Eagle River in place and converted both to pedestrian and bicycle use. The US-12 bridge is a three-span concrete camelback in the semirural setting of Mottville, a small town in southwest Michigan. A pleasant roadside park and bike paths provide access to the bridge. At the M-26 bridge, in the Eagle River Historic District in the scenic Keewenaw Peninsula, MDOT built a modern wooden arch bridge next to the historic Warren deck truss, contributing to the idyllic setting. Site development includes a roadside park near the historic bridge, which pedestrians use as a viewing platform for the dam and falls upstream.

In both settings, it was possible to relocate the roadway a short distance from the historic bridge. This enabled MDOT to improve the alignment of each road with the new bridge and maintain the historic bridge on the highway system as part of a roadside park. MDOT and Ionia County are also proposing a similar treatment for White's Bridge, one of only three historic covered timber bridges in Michigan.

3. *Rehabilitate without affecting the historic integrity of the bridge.* This alternative allows us to keep the historic bridge in service as a bridge on a highway while bringing it up to modern standards for safety and efficiency. Many historic bridges are structurally deficient; that is, they are simply worn out. They often cannot be repaired without destroying their historic integrity, either because the techniques used to construct them are no longer practiced, the parts are no longer available, or the repairs are so extensive that the bridge, if repaired, would no longer be an original but a replica of its former self.

Other historic bridges are functionally obsolete; they do not meet current standards because they are too narrow, do not have crash-resistant railings, do not meet current load limits, or do not meet other current standards. Until recently, if bridges were to be repaired with federal funds, they had to be brought up to current standards to ensure their safety—not an easy task. Through-truss bridges or concrete camelback bridges generally cannot be widened because of their interconnected members without destroying them. Others cannot be economically widened, especially small pony truss bridges in rural areas. More recently, under the Intermodel Surface Transportation Efficiency Act (December 1991), state highway departments received greater authority to approve historic bridge rehabilitation projects where the rehabilitated bridge does not meet current standards. This may prove especially important for rural highway bridges.

MDOT has had significant success in maintaining and rehabilitating some of its historic bridges. The department has extensively reconstructed several bridges to meet modern standards for safety and maintained them on the highway system, while preserving their historic integrity. Although there is some flexibility in applying current standards to historic bridges, railings must be crash resistant. Modern bridge railings must deflect an out-of-control car or truck and prevent it from going over the side of the bridge.

MDOT uses two strategies to install crash-resistant railings on historic bridges. The first involves building new sidewalk structures that retain the original historic railings and installing new crash-resistant railings between the roadway and the sidewalks. This method was used on the US-2 (Cut River) bridge in Mackinac County and on the M-55 (Cooley) bridge in Manistee County. The second strategy is to design a new composite railing with crash-resistant segments on the street side and the original historic panels on the outside. In both cases, MDOT is able to maintain the historic exterior appearance of the bridge while upgrading the railings to meet modern standards.

Both the Cut River and Cooley bridges are cantilevered steel deck truss bridges in dramatic settings and attract much pedestrian traffic to enjoy the views. Only a painted line separated the sidewalks on these rural state highway bridges from the traffic. To provide wider traffic lanes and improve pedestrian and traffic safety, MDOT cantilevered new sidewalks out along the bridge deck and carefully designed the steel supporting the sidewalks to match the existing design and steel work. The department built a crash-resistant, see-through tube railing between the traffic lanes and the sidewalk. This separated the traffic and pedestrians and provided a crash-resistant barrier that meets current standards for cars. MDOT regalvanized the original exterior railing panels, good enough for pedestrian protection, and placed them on new, replicated posts. As a result, the two bridges retain their original general appearance, meet current standards, and will remain on the state highway system for years to come.

The department has reconstructed other bridges as well. At the US-31 bridge over the Manistee River in Manistee County, a Scherzer bascule bridge, MDOT restored and updated the operator's house, upgraded the railings, replaced the steel grating on the deck, and otherwise restored and modernized the bridge. The department also helped restore the Second Street bridge in Allegan, Allegan County, in 1982, well before all the current preservation requirements were in place; the Dix Avenue bascule bridge in Wayne County; and the Bridge Street bridge in Portland, Ionia County, a steel through truss restored in 1990 for its centennial.

Through the creative efforts of its environmental, design, maintenance, and construction staffs, MDOT completed extensive repairs on these bridges, while preserving their historic integrity and returning them to active service.

4. *Reuse on a new site*. Some bridges can be moved. Truss bridges, both through and pony, are especially adaptable to this preservation strategy. They can either be moved intact, if the distance is not too great, or carefully dismantled and rebuilt. The Surface Transportation and Uniform Relocation Assistance Act of 1987 promotes this approach by allowing the Federal Highway Administration to contribute the cost of demolition toward relocation. The law even *required* highway agencies to advertise the availability for relocation of any historic bridge it was proposing to replace.

MDOT has successfully moved several bridges with the help of local highway agencies. Most notably, the Dehmel Road bridge in Saginaw County is to be reerected in Frankenmuth. In addition, the department has relocated the East Sheridan Road bridge in Saginaw County, part of the North Park Street bridge in Kent County, and the Belleville bridge in Wayne County; however, this alternative is often difficult to accomplish effectively. Few people or organizations are willing to take these bridges even when they can be economically moved. The new owner must assume all liability for the historic bridge and restore it to its original condition. Although other states have had some greater success in this, the actual number of bridges saved by moving is small.

5. *Record before demolition*. If there is no other option, a historian prepares documentation on the historic bridge before demolition occurs. This documentation consists of photographs of the bridge in its current condition, copies of historic photographs of the bridge, plans (or, if available, copies of the original bridge construction plans), and a written history of the bridge. This documentation becomes part of the Historic American Engineering Record Collection in the Library of Congress. This has been the fate of many bridges identified as historically significant. They are photographed, the documentation filed, and the bridge torn down. At the present rate of attrition, only a few of the once-common types of bridges will be standing anywhere in Michigan, and those that remain will be in roadside parks, or on rarely used country, closed, and inaccessible roads.

There are many obstacles to saving historic bridges. It requires more paperwork, time, and money to move a historic bridge than it does to demolish it. This process can take up to two years. If MDOT can show that there is no alternative, an historic bridge can be recorded, demolished, and replaced within a year; thus, this becomes a more attractive alternative.

Time and money can be saved by requiring less effort if a bridge is to be saved. Right now, any options that save a bridge by going around it or moving it, require at least as much documentation as tearing it down. This is frustrating especially at the local level. Reducing the amount of paperwork required to save bridges is an incentive that does not add to the cost of these projects. To encourage the preservation of historic bridges, there must be some advantage to the state or county highway agency beyond the regulatory requirements and moral obligations, especially when the local public does not vigorously support preservation.

On a brighter note, some historic bridges disappearing in Michigan are those we can most afford to lose. They are mostly small rural bridges with plenty of candidates to take their place on the historic bridge list.

Although a few of the more unique bridges have already disappeared, Michigan's larger and monumental bridges, most of which are on the state highway system, are in good repair and will remain in service for a long time. Where local communities recognize bridges as historic—as in the cases of the three covered bridges and the truss bridges in Allegan, Grand Rapids, and Portland—preservation is a much easier goal to achieve. The future holds little hope for most historic bridges without strong local advocacy. MDOT and the Bureau of History must reassess the bridges not yet included in the historic bridge list because they were not old enough, to determine if some of these should be placed on the list of eligible bridges to replace those lost to demolition. Special effort should be made to include those with a reasonable chance of survival, given the bridge's condition and location or a strong local desire to support its preservation. Targeting these "preservable" bridges helps

ensure that at least some of them will remain for future generations to view and appreciate.

The new federal transportation law, the Intermodal Surface Transportation Efficiency Act of 1991, has added greatly to the Michigan Department of Transportation's ability to preserve historic bridges. There may even be funds available to help with maintaining these structures. The Bureau of History and the Michigan Department of Transportation are developing a new preservation plan to take advantage of this new law. Also, the Bureau of History has determined that the list of historic bridges identified in the bridge inventory completed in 1985 is no longer valid because so many bridges have been lost and the criteria for determining their historic significance have changed. The bridge inventory will be revised in 1993 and incorporated into a new preservation plan.

Acknowledgments

This book springs from my work on Michigan's historic engineering sites that began more than fifteen years ago. I first came to appreciate Michigan's remarkable variety of surviving historic highway bridges while conducting an inventory of the state's historic engineering and industrial sites in 1975–1977 for the Historic American Engineering Record (HAER) of the United States National Park Service and the Bureau of History, Michigan Department of State. I subsequently completed an extensive study of Michigan's historic highway bridges for the Michigan Department of Transportation (MDOT) and the Bureau of History (BOH) in 1984–1985.

Martha M. Bigelow, director of the Bureau of History and Michigan's state historic preservation officer (SHPO) in 1971–1990, and Kathryn B. Eckert, Michigan's SHPO since 1992, have vigorously supported my work on Michigan's historic sites over the years. Eric Delony from HAER did much to help launch the Michigan Historic Highway Bridge Study. In the course of that project, Janet Kreger and Robert Christensen from the BOH staff provided much assistance and advice. Professor Donald C. Jackson of Lafayette College, a respected historic bridge expert formerly with HAER, was an outside consultant for the bridge study and continues to serve as my bridge guru, providing me with engineering and spiritual guidance.

This book would not have happened without the hard work and commitment of many individuals and institutions. Philip P. Mason, editor of the Great Lakes Books Series and my colleague at Wayne State University, has been a strong advocate of this book from the start. Arthur B. Evans, the director of the Wayne State University Press, and Basil C. Hedrick, former director of Museums, Archeology and Publications for the Bureau of History, have offered unwavering support during the book's long gestation. Paul W. McAllister from the Bureau of

Transportation Planning of the Michigan Department of Transportation wrote the foreword, organized the production of the graphic illustrations and many of the photographs, and provided constant encouragement. I am grateful for his assistance. I would like to thank Saralee Howard-Filler, former managing editor of the Bureau of History's Book Program, for her painstaking and patient work on the early phases of this book. The financial assistance of the Mackinac Bridge Authority is also gratefully acknowledged.

Scores of librarians and archivists helped me locate information on Michigan's highway bridges. LeRoy Barnett and John Curry at the State Archives of Michigan have been particularly patient and generous with their time. David A. Simmons from the Ohio Historical Society steered me to materials on Ohio truss bridge manufacturers that built many of Michigan's bridges. Simmons was also a principal contributor to the Ohio Historic Bridge Inventory (1983), a model study.

Several more specific debts must be acknowledged. I am indebted to Sudhakar Kulkarni from the Design Division of MDOT, who compiled information on Michigan bridge projects after World War II. Robert O. Christensen and Donald C. Jackson generously allowed the use of their private collections of postcards of Michigan historic bridges. Carla Anderson photographically copied the postcards and other historic views. MDOT's Photography Laboratory staff took field photographs of existing bridges and completed photocopy work as well. I am especially grateful to Linda Bosheff, the photography laboratory coordinator, and staff photographers Steve Bollinger, Tim Burke, Jim LeMay, and Dell Phillips. Gary A. Eiseler from MDOT's Graphic Design Unit produced the attractive line drawings that appear in the book. Gary would not have been able to do this work without the full cooperation of his supervisor, Jim Grugett. Finally, Lynn H. Trease from Wayne State University Press edited the book with great efficiency and skill.

I am of course solely responsible for any errors of fact or interpretation that may have found their way into this volume.

Introduction

Michigan's highway bridges are perhaps the state's most common historic resource, but they are also the most threatened by change. They are an important element in our individual and collective lives and a common feature of the "built environment," which we too often take for granted. Bridges are one of the most purely utilitarian historic resources of modern industrial society. They became old and derelict and dangerous all too quickly; increased traffic volumes and loads contributed to their premature decline. We often view them as short-lived, disposable features of the cultural landscape.

This book attempts to identify Michigan's historically significant highway bridges within the broader contexts of American bridge design and construction in the nineteenth and twentieth centuries. It is a revised and updated version of an extensive study of Michigan highway bridges completed in 1984–1985 for the Michigan Department of Transportation (MDOT) and the Bureau

of History (BOH) of the Michigan Department of State. Michigan has nearly 11,000 highway bridges, with 4,500 of them on interstate highways and state trunklines. The historic bridge study of 1984–1985, focusing on about 600 bridges, concluded that 140 of these were historically significant. These were in turn determined eligible for listing on the National Register of Historic Places. That group of bridges, now reduced by replacements to about 105, is the primary focus of this volume. That number is likely to be less than one hundred by the time this book appears. Michigan also has thousands of railroad bridges within its borders; more than one hundred of these have historical significance. This volume excludes railroad bridges, which deserve a separate study.

Although Michigan has notable monumental bridges, considered in chapter 5, most bridges delineated in this volume are "ordinary highway bridges." They range in age from White's Bridge (1867), a timber covered bridge, to the Zilwaukee Bridge (1988), a post-tensioned, segmental, box girder structure. The Mackinac Straits Bridge is easily the largest in the state, slightly more than five miles long, including approaches, but most bridges are less than 200 feet long, with many considerably shorter.

The foreword examined the difficult challenge of preserving historic bridges from the perspective of the bridge engineer and transportation planner. Paul McAllister described Michigan's successful efforts to preserve some of its historic highway bridges, while bemoaning the loss of many other bridges. Chapter 1, emphasizing the design and construction of bridges, presents a general history of Michigan's transportation system in the nineteenth and twentieth centuries. Chapter 2 discusses the major bridge types commonly built in the United States in the nineteenth and early twentieth centuries, and includes examples of each type found in Michigan; these include masonry arch, timber truss, and the most common nineteenth-century bridge type, the metal truss.

Chapter 3 considers bridge design in the late nineteenth and twentieth centuries, including steel girder designs; moveable bridges of all types; steel arch, steel cantilever, and steel suspension designs; concrete arch bridges; and finally, concrete girder bridges. To aid the reader interested in visiting the historic highway bridges of Michigan, the bridges described in this book are numbered consecutively starting in Chapter 2. The numbers appear on regional maps of Michigan, found in Appendix A, and serve as a guide to the approximate locations of the bridges. The tourist in search of historic bridges still needs state and county road maps to find his or her way to the bridge site. Chapter 4 summarizes the history of bridge design and construction in Michigan since World War II, with emphasis on design innovations, while Chapter 5 focuses on Michigan's half dozen monumental bridges. Appendix B identifies the builders of metal truss bridges within Michigan, and a bibliography directs the reader to additional source materials.

Perhaps this book will encourage the citizens of Michigan to work even harder to carry out the sentiments expressed in the Federal Surface Transportation Act of 1987:

Congress hereby finds and declares it to be in the national interest to encourage the rehabilitation, reuse and preservation of bridges significant in American history, architecture, engineering, and culture. Historic bridges are important links to our past, serve as safe and vital transportation routes to the present, and can represent significant resources for the future.

CHAPTER **1**

Michigan's Transportation Systems in the Nineteenth and Twentieth Centuries: From Wagon Paths to Superhighways

For nearly half a century the designing, letting and construction of highway bridges have been synonymous with ignorance, cupidity, and graft; and it is only lately that there has been any genuine improvement in the highway bridge business.

J. A. L. WADDELL, in
Bridge Engineering, 1916

Michigan's rapid economic development and population growth in the nineteenth century resulted from the growth of its major industries at the time—agriculture, lumber, and mining. The white population of Michigan, a paltry 30,000 in 1830, jumped to about 750,000 by 1860. By the turn of the century, state population had grown to 2.4 million, and Detroit—Michigan's major manufacturing center and largest city—had a population of nearly 300,000.[1]

Waterways were the first important avenues of transportation and trade in Michigan. The Great Lakes provided long-distance movement of low-value, bulky freight more than a century before the first railroads, and they have remained an important means of transportation throughout the twentieth century. Michigan's major rivers—including the Detroit, St. Clair, Saginaw, Grand, Kalamazoo, Huron, and Raisin—were major commercial arteries. As a result, crossings often had to be made with moveable bridges, to avoid disrupting river traffic.

The railroad opened Michigan to development beginning in the 1840s and soon became the predominant system for transporting passengers and most freight. The Michigan Southern Railroad began in Monroe in 1843 and extended through the southernmost tier of counties, while the Michigan Central Railroad went from Detroit to Kalamazoo through the second tier of counties. Both lines reached Chicago in 1852. A third line, the Detroit and Milwaukee Railroad, ran from Detroit to Pontiac in 1843 and eventually reached Grand Haven in 1858. The growth of the state's railroad system after the Civil War was extensive and chaotic. By the turn of the century, Michigan had more than 8,000 miles of mainline track, controlled by more than two hundred distinct companies.

◀ Kingpost timber bridge over the Ontonagon River at Watersmeet. Courtesy of Robert O. Christensen.

The railroad, serving all but the most remote villages, was the premier inland transportation system.[2]

Michigan's roads, such as they were in the nineteenth century, mainly fed the railroad lines. Plank roads had achieved some popularity in the 1840s and 1850s, but virtually all the road mileage before 1900 consisted of dirt roads, which became mud roads for several months each year. Local authorities built and maintained the roads through a "statute labor" system. In lieu of taxes, residents, using inadequate equipment and materials, worked several days a year on local roads, usually under the supervision of a local official.[3]

▲ Timber through truss bridge over the Huron River at Vassar. Courtesy of Robert O. Christensen.

Timber bridge (1861) over the Muskegon River in Big Rapids, Mecosta County.
At the time of the photograph (1871), sawmills were still in full operation.

There was little involvement by state or even county governments until the end of the nineteenth century. One exception was an 1883 Michigan law that gave people using wide (larger than 3.5-inch) tires on their wagons a rebate of one-fourth of their highway tax assessment each year. Narrow tires destroyed even the best roads in short order. In 1893, Michigan passed legislation enabling counties to establish road commissions and issue bonds for highway improvements, but few counties did so until the automobile era began in earnest about ten years later. By that time, Michigan had roughly 70,000 miles of public wagon roads. About 10 percent of the total mileage had gravel surfacing and less than 1 percent had cobblestone, brick, or macadam surfaces.[4]

▲ Town lattice truss bridge over Thornapple River, Kent County.
Courtesy of State Archives of Michigan.

▶ Fallasburg Bridge (1871)
over the Flat River, Kent
County. Courtesy of MDOT.

Pearl Street Bridge (1858) over the Grand River, Grand Rapids. This six-span structure was 620 feet long and remained in use until 1886. Photograph (1874) courtesy of State Archives of Michigan.

Highway Bridge Construction: Politics and Economics

Local units of government, including counties, built most highway bridges in the United States. Local officials—often unpaid, part-time public servants—decided the strength, type, and cost of bridges in their jurisdiction, many times without the technical information or expertise they needed. Until about 1875, most substantial bridges were timber trusses, both covered and open, with a handful of stone arch designs. The popularity of timber bridges is not surprising, given Michigan's role as a major lumbering state through the 1890s. Public officials could use local craftsmen and contractors to design and build bridges with materials

23

Masonry arch bridge, location unknown. Courtesy of Robert O. Christensen.

obtained locally. For example, two Kent County men, Jared N. Brazee and Joseph H. Walker, built at least four covered bridges in Kent and Ionia counties between 1862 and 1870. If the builders remained in the area, they could not avoid responsibility for their work.[5]

The growing popularity of the metal truss after about 1875 changed the way local governments acquired bridges. In Michigan, virtually all the bridges built dur-ing the last quarter of the nineteenth century were metal trusses designed and fabricated by bridge companies located in other states. Local officials had to make technical decisions about bridge specifications, including the loading requirements and var-ious design options.

Recognizing these difficulties, Alfred P. Boller, a civil engineer, wrote his *Practical Treatise on the Construction of Iron Highway Bridges for the Use of Town Committees* in 1876, as a way of giving public officials a "short course" in bridge engineering. He explained how trusses worked, described the major truss types, and included a brief descrip-tion of girder bridges. Boller suggested load-ing specifications determined by the length of the span and the type of traffic carried. He also made suggestions about the letting of bridge contracts, including the requirement that all parties submitting bids provide draw-ings and calculations of stress.[6]

▲ County officials responsible for building the Bridge Street Bridge (1890) over the Grand River in the city of Portland, Ionia County. Courtesy of MDOT.

▶ Goodwin Bridge over the Grand River in Portland, Ionia County, "as it looked a few hours before the ice and water swept it down stream." Courtesy of State Archives of Michigan.

The public officials who awarded bridge contracts had to consider the initial cost of the structure, its durability and maintenance costs, and safety. Contemporary engineers generally agreed that bridges ought to be designed to carry from four to six times the maximum expected load, to provide a wide margin of safety. Nevertheless, bridge failures occurred with frightening frequency.[7]

The most deadly bridge failure was the collapse of a railroad bridge near Ashtabula, Ohio, on December 29, 1876: a passenger train crashed into the stream below, killing ninety-three people. The railroad's president, an amateur bridge designer with no engineering training, had designed this particular deck truss. But bridges failed for reasons other than poor design. Many fell victim to floods or ice or were rammed by locomotives or ships. Inferior iron or steel was sometimes the culprit, and on more than one occasion simple overloading brought disaster. One Iowa span of 160 feet collapsed when a cattleman drove a hefty herd over it.[8]

Waddell's *The Designing of Ordinary Iron Highway Bridges* (1884) offers a detailed description of the way local governments awarded bridge contracts in the nineteenth century. County or local officials would advertise for bids in newspapers and by circu-

Small bowstring truss bridge over the Huron River, Dexter, Washtenaw County. Courtesy of State Archives of Michigan.

lar to the major bridge companies, who would submit a bid by mail or through an agent. Usually, a public meeting followed, where the public officials examined the bids and awarded a contract. The fundamental weakness in this system was the lack of engineering knowledge by both the public officials and the bridge salesmen. The specifications could be sufficiently ambiguous to tempt the low bidder to cut corners to increase his profits. Waddell argued that bidders should produce their own detailed specifications to submit with their bids. He believed that public officials should hire an independent bridge engineer to write the specifications, examine the bids, and award the contract. He preferred to eliminate the public meeting altogether because it was costly and unproductive.[9]

The successful bidder had its engineering department produce a set of drawings for the bridge or adapt one of the firm's standard designs. Most major structural members were ordered from a rolling mill and then cut, punched, and reamed to specification in

Small through truss bridge over the Tobacco River, Gladwin County.
Courtesy of Donald C. Jackson.

the bridge company shop. Some larger bridge firms had their own forge departments to make eyebars, rivets, and pins.   The firm normally fit the structural members together in the shop but then shipped the various pieces of the bridge, with an accompanying "erection plan," to the construction site. Company officials supervised the erection, using their own workers or local labor. A gang of six to eight men seemed sufficient to build a small through truss of less than 100 feet and place it on its abutments, but larger crews of thirty or forty men might be needed for bridges of 300 feet or more.[10]

In the second half of the nineteenth century, the iron truss bridge and specialized bridge manufacturing firms emerged simultaneously. Sometimes, an inventor who held patents on a truss turned entrepreneur and established a firm to produce the patented design or patented features. Bridge companies appeared in large numbers practically overnight, but were mostly small and short-lived.[11]

According to a directory of bridge firms compiled by historian Victor Darnell, roughly 600 companies in thirty-eight states operated during the period from 1840 to 1900. They were located in a few eastern and midwestern states, led by Pennsylvania (100 firms), Ohio (87), New York (77), and Illinois (62). These numbers are deceptive, though, because many firms simply assem-

Two views of a large three-span bowstring arch through truss bridge over the Grand River in Saranac, Ionia County. Courtesy of Robert O. Christensen.

Bowstring arch bridge, 160 feet long, assembled in downtown Owosso, Shiawassee County, January 1895. Men are moving the bridge on rollers to its location on the Shiawassee River, more than one mile away. Courtesy of State Archives of Michigan.

bled bridges designed or fabricated by others, and most firms on the list survived for less than five years. Only about fifty bridge companies produced a substantial number of bridges nationally in the nineteenth century. Darnell listed nine Michigan bridge firms, for example, but only the Detroit Bridge and Iron Works (1863–1901) was a significant producer.[12]

The market for metal truss bridges appeared more competitive than it really was. A few bridge companies sold their products nationally, but most firms could not submit bids on small highway bridges, fabricate, and then ship the product long distances and still make a profit. The bridge industry served a set of regional markets, rather than a national market. For Michigan, I have identified the builders of 210 highway bridges, not all of which are still standing (see Appendix B). Bridge companies based

Man practicing headstands on upper chord of bridge over the Tittabawassee River at Midland (1908). Courtesy of State Archives of Michigan.

outside the Great Lakes states of Michigan, Ohio, Indiana, Illinois, and Wisconsin accounted for only 13 of the 210 bridges. Two firms, the Groton Bridge and Manufacturing Company of Groton, New York, and the Penn Bridge Works of Beaver Falls, Pennsylvania, built five bridge each in Michigan. Bridge firms specialized in particular styles of bridges and developed particular geographic orientations as well. The Champion Bridge Company, located at Wilmington, Ohio, in the southwest corner of the state, built about 5,500 bridges between 1884 and 1927, but not a single one in Michigan. Champion not only built a large number of bridges in Ohio, but it also had enormous sales in West Virginia, Kentucky, Tennessee, and several states of the Deep South.[13]

Individual bridge lettings seemed competitive, with ten or twelve bids commonplace, but bridge manufacturing firms engaged in extensive price fixing and other collusive practices from about 1880 until the end of the century. Midwestern bridge companies created "pools," whereby they divided the market by rigging or manipulating the so-called competitive bidding system. Sometimes, the "competitors" shared bidding information to assure that each firm received a certain share of contracts awarded. On other occasions, the firms allowed bidding to proceed competitively, but members of the pool then shared in the profits of the successful bidder. In any case, artificially inflated prices and profits resulted from the pools.[14]

One irony of the Sherman Anti-Trust Act

New bridge over the Tittabawassee River at Midland (1907).
Courtesy of State Archives of Michigan.

(1890), as interpreted by the Supreme Court, was the prohibition of "pools" as a "restraint of trade," but no similar condemnation of mergers. One result was the formation in 1900 of the American Bridge Company, which became a subsidiary of the United States Steel Corporation a year later. American Bridge involved the merger of twenty-four substantial bridge producers, with half the industry's fabricating capacity. The addition of several other bridge companies by 1903 produced one dominant firm.[15]

The domination of the metal truss bridge industry by a handful of firms was as true in Michigan as it was nationally. Forty firms constructed Michigan's 210 metal truss bridges with known builders, but only eight of them were Michigan firms that accounted for fourteen bridges. Four out-of-state firms dominate the list: the Wrought Iron Bridge Company (50 bridges), King Bridge Company (38), and the Massillon Bridge Company (21), all from Ohio, and the Joliet Bridge and Iron Company (21) from Illinois.

The Twentieth Century: The Automobile Age

The state's economic development and population growth in the twentieth century largely resulted from the growth of manufacturing in Michigan, particularly automobile manufacturing and related industries. Michigan's population jumped from about 2.4 million in 1900 to 5.3 million by 1940. Detroit's population rose from about 300,000 to 1.6 million during the same period, an increase accounting for nearly half the state's total population growth. The rapid growth of automobile sales in the nation and in Michigan drastically altered the state's economic base and, with short lags, its transportation system as well. American automobile production, a mere 24,000 units in 1905, jumped to 1.9 million in 1920 and then to 3.7 million by 1925, with Model T Fords accounting for more than half the sales between 1908 and 1925.[16]

Railroads continued to handle a large volume of passenger traffic into the early 1920s before beginning their long decline. Michigan's railroads carried more than 23 million passengers in 1914, mostly over long distances. For a brief period, the state had an extensive system of electric interurban lines (light rail). The first line opened in 1890 and linked Ann Arbor and Ypsilanti; this permitted, among other things, faster movement between the all-male University of Michigan and the all-female Michigan State

Normal School. The success of that first line set off a boom in interurban lines, and by 1918, eighteen companies operated more than one thousand miles of interurban lines in southern Michigan. Detroit was the hub of the system, with spokes reaching out to Toledo, Port Huron, Bay City, Kalamazoo, Grand Rapids, and Muskegon. The interurban lines connected to the major city streetcar systems and often shared common ownership. At their peak in 1918, the combined interurban and streetcar systems carried an astonishing total of 380 million passengers.[17]

The interurbans fell victim to the competition of the private automobile, and between 1924 and the end of the decade virtually the entire interurban system disappeared. Even the railroad network was in a state of decline, with mainline track shrinking from about 9,000 miles in 1915 to 7,300 miles by the beginning of the Second World War. The growth of automobile ownership in Michigan, improvements in the state's roads, and the decline of

the steam railroad and electric interurban passenger service went hand in hand.[18]

Michigan had only about 3,000 automobiles in 1905, but it registered 413,000 in 1920, and automobile registrations climbed to more than 1.4 million by 1929, the eve of the Great Depression. Private bus operators, providing even more competition to rail travel and adding pressure to improve the highways, also began intercity and interstate service. By 1925, about 100 companies with more than 500 buses carried more than 16 million passengers statewide. The nineteenth century was the age of the railroad, the horse-drawn vehicle, and water transportation, while the twentieth century, at least from the 1910s on, has been the age of the automobile, the bus, and the truck. When the transition to the automobile began in earnest after the turn of the century, Michigan quickly adopted new approaches for the design, construction, and financing of the state's highways and bridges.[19]

Horatio S. Earle, Michigan state highway commissioner, 1905–1909. Photograph taken in 1901. Courtesy of State Archives of Michigan.

The Structure and Financing of Highway Improvements

When the transition to the automobile began in earnest after the turn of the century, Michigan quickly adopted new approaches to the design, construction, and financing of state highways and bridges. The state government, through the State Highway Department, became the major vehicle for road and bridge improvements. The department directly built a large number of roads and bridges, but more important, stimulated county road commissions and local governments to improve roads with a variety of methods including financial aid and technical assistance. Although considerable federal involvement and influence was already evident before the Second World War, this remained an era in which most highway funding, engineering, and planning took place at the state and local level.

The initial drive for state participation in highway improvements had to overcome several major legal and political obstacles. In 1837, during the early days of statehood, Michigan enacted legislation providing for state aid for "internal improvements," specifically for two canals and three railroads. The state government borrowed $5 million and gave away millions of acres of public lands for these projects, which were pathetic failures. The entire experiment in state aid was a disaster, with corruption, incompetence, and poor planning contributing to the fiasco. One unfortunate result, however, was the outright prohibition on state aid for internal improvements in Michigan's 1850 Constitution. In addition, the state's farmers, a potent political force, saw higher taxes as the only result of road improvements and became the most vehement opponents of state involvement.[20]

The initial impetus for better roads came from bicyclists. The League of American Wheelmen (LAW), established in 1880 to promote cyclists' rights to use public streets and highways, became an effective lobby for better highways beginning in the 1890s. The Michigan division of the LAW, established in 1883, was instrumental in getting legislation passed in 1893 to permit counties to create road commissions. Horatio S. Earle, an early advocate of better roads and Michigan's first state highway commissioner, was active in the Michigan division of the LAW, became its chief consul in 1899, and then served as president of the league in 1902. He won election to the Michigan State Senate in November 1901, largely on a "good-roads" platform, and began a series of moves that led to the establishment of the State Highway Department a few years later.[21]

In 1901, Earle convinced both houses of the Michigan legislature to create a joint committee to study the road problem and to make recommendations. Governor Aaron Bliss made Earle chairman of the committee, which issued its report in 1903. The com-

State Reward Bridge Plaque (1924), Pine Island Drive Bridge over the Rogue [*sic*] River, Kent County. Courtesy of MDOT.

mittee, urging the establishment of a state highway department and state aid for roads, recognized that this would require a constitutional amendment. Shortly thereafter, the legislature passed a bill creating a State Highway Department, which had educational functions only. Bliss appointed Earle to the post of state commissioner of highways in June 1903, but the state attorney general immediately ruled the legislation unconstitutional so no funds could be spent. Earle nevertheless worked as Michigan's unpaid, "unconstitutional" highway commissioner until the voters approved a constitutional amendment on April 3, 1905, to permit state aid for roads. Earle became Michigan's first "constitutional" state highway commissioner and held the post for a single term of four years.[22]

The State Reward Law of 1905 established the State Highway Department and the system used by the state to provide financial aid to counties and townships for road construction. Having established the basic organization of the State Highway Department, the legislation required that the deputy state highway commissioner be "a competent civil engineer." It provided for state aid to county and local governments for road construction that met the department's standards, with "rewards" ranging from $250 per mile for gravel roads to $1,000 per mile for macadam construction. The legislation provided $20,000 for aid in the first year and $50,000 for the second.[23]

Although an 1893 act permitted the establishment of county road commissions that could issue bonds for road repairs or construction, only eighteen counties (out of eighty-three) had done so by 1905; virtually all of these were located in northern Michigan or in the upper peninsula. The requirement of a two-thirds vote of the County Board of Supervisors simply to place the question before the voters was largely responsible for this poor showing. In 1905 Earle convinced the legislature to amend the 1893 Act to allow a small number of voters, through a petition, to place the county road commission question on the ballot. Even with this change, the establishment of county road commissions went slowly. In 1910, thirty-two counties had done so, and by 1916, the number had jumped to fifty-nine.[24]

The highway department's role in improving the state road system expanded enormously between 1905 and the late 1930s. The State Trunk Line Act of 1913 initially established a system of about 3,000 miles of state trunk line highways, and provided $500,000 in funding for the first two years, to be distributed in the form of additional state rewards. By 1919, the state had already completed or upgraded more than 2,000 miles of highways and one hundred bridges. The trunkline system expanded as the legislature authorized additional mileage, so by 1933, for example, the system had grown to 8,548 miles.[25]

◀ Frank F. Rogers, deputy highway commissioner, 1905–1913; highway commissioner, 1913–1929. Photograph taken in 1917. Courtesy of State Archives of Michigan.

▶ Murray D. Van Wagoner, state highway commissioner, 1933–1940. Photograph taken in 1933. Courtesy of State Archives of Michigan.

Federal funding also aided road improvements. The Federal Road Aid Act, passed by Congress in 1916, provided $75 million in federal funds over five years, to be given to the states on a fifty-fifty matching basis. Michigan began participating in the program 1917. Although federal aid was a significant part of the funding used for roads and bridges in the 1910s and 1920s, it did not yet play the decisive role it would after the Second World War. Federal aid accounted for only 16 percent of the total $2 billion spent on highway improvements in Michigan from 1910 to 1946.[26]

A significant shift in the philosophy of highway financing took place in 1919, when Michigan voters authorized the legislature to issue up to $50 million in bonds for road improvements. From 1917 through 1924, the state completed its first major road building campaign, spending about $81 million in federal aid along with the $50 million raised through the bond issue. The trunkline system

had grown to 6,600 miles, while the state improved thousands of miles of other roads.[27]

The highway department enjoyed the benefits of continuity among its top officials through the 1930s. Horatio Earle was commissioner from 1905 to 1909, followed by Townsend A. Ely from 1909 to 1913, but then Frank F. Rogers, who had been a deputy commissioner since 1905, held the top post from 1913 until early 1929. The governor appointed the first two commissioners, but after 1913, they ran for election to a four-year term. Grover Dillman, the deputy commissioner from 1922 to 1928, replaced Rogers in January 1929 and served until July 1933. Murray van Wagoner then served as commissioner until June 1940.[28]

Highway Bridge Construction Comes of Age

During the first eight years of its existence, the State Highway Department had little

direct involvement in bridge design or construction, beyond occasionally giving advice to local officials. Two pieces of legislation radically changed this. The State Trunk Line Act of 1913 required the State Highway Department to build and maintain all trunk line bridges, entirely at state expense, while the State Reward Act of 1919 required the department to pay half the cost and to supervise the construction of all bridges on State Reward Roads. With the passage of the first act, the department appointed its first bridge engineer, C. V. Dewart, to head the new bridge division.

During the two-year fiscal period ending July 1, 1914, the state built only one trunk line bridge, a six-span concrete girder structure, 246 feet long, over the Peshekee River near Michigamme in Marquette County. In the next three fiscal periods, trunk line bridge construction accelerated, with 34 bridges finished in 1914–1916, another 40 in 1916–1918, and 85 completed in 1918–

Standard concrete "camelback" girder bridge, over the Manistique River at Germfask, Schoolcraft County. Courtesy of Robert O. Christensen.

1920. The numbers swelled in the early 1920s, with of 114 built in 1920–1922 and 156 in 1922–1924.[29]

Dewart quickly developed a set of standard bridge plans to use on the trunk line system and to supply to local governments upon request. He began in 1915 with concrete girder designs because they could be built by local contractors employing carpenters and unskilled laborers, used readily available materials, required little maintenance, and, because of their massive size, provided a wide margin of safety. Initially, Dewart developed plans for concrete girder spans of 30, 35, and 40 feet, but he added 45- and 50-foot spans in 1916, all with an 18-foot roadway. These concrete girder bridges, with their unique "camelback" design, became well known throughout the state as "Dewart's tunnels." The State Highway Department developed standard plans for both concrete and steel pipe culverts, concrete abutments and floors for steel girder spans, and steel Warren pony truss spans ranging in length from 50 to 120 feet, varying by 5-foot intervals.[30]

Standard concrete "camelback" girder bridge, with sidewalk, over the
Indian River in Indian River, Cheboygan County.
Courtesy of Robert O. Christensen.

Standard concrete girder bridge, US-23 north of Standish, Arenac County.
Courtesy of Robert O. Christensen.

Michigan was not alone in moving toward standard designs for culverts and short-span bridges. The Illinois Highway Commission had the burdensome task of satisfying hundreds of requests for bridge plans made every year, as noted in a publication released in 1912. By 1917, Illinois and Kentucky were among the earliest midwestern states to use standard bridge designs. Several national publications discussed Michigan's efforts at least a year earlier, one indication of Dewart's pioneering work. In part because it used standard designs, the Michigan Highway Department was able to build a large number of bridges economically. It contracted for 240 bridges during the six years ending in July 1920; of these, more than half (137) were concrete girders, 32 were concrete arches (*not* standardized), and 28 were pony trusses.[31]

Much of the impetus for standardization came from Washington, beginning with the Federal Aid Road Act of 1916, which specified that bridges on the federal aid system had to be at least sixteen feet wide, with a minimum clearance of fourteen feet. The U.S. Bureau of Public Roads, which administered federal highway

Michigan Highway Department concrete arch bridge over the Rapid
River, Antrim County. Courtesy of Robert O. Christensen.

programs before the Second World War, did
much to encourage standardization of
materials and design on the nation's highway system. The move toward standardization and minimum technical specifications was
gradual in Michigan, where the highway
department did not release a published set of
minimum standards until 1926. The federal
government simply encouraged a continua-
tion of a trend that had already begun under
Dewart.[32]

The same basic pattern continued under
C. A. Melick, the State Highway Department's bridge engineer from early 1918 to
June 1932. Starting in 1920, the department
adopted a steel riveted Parker truss as its standard pony truss design, with plans provided
for trusses of 100, 110, and 120 feet. In the
early 1920s, the reinforced concrete (camelback) through girder was by far the most
popular standard design. By 1923, plans
were available for spans of 45, 60, 75, and
90 feet, to provide roadway widths of 18,
20, 22, and 24 feet. These girder bridges,
with their massive concrete camelback form,
are found only in Michigan and the Province
of Ontario.[33]

Standard steel Pratt through truss bridge, US-23 over the Au Sable River at
Au Sable, Iosco County, ca. 1920. Courtesy of Robert O. Christensen.

Standard steel riveted Parker through truss bridge, M-33, M-72 over the Au Sable
River at Mio, Oscoda County. Courtesy of Robert O. Christensen.

The department's bridge engineers not only did innovative design work on individual bridges, but they also departed from standard practices in less exotic ways and received recognition for their work in the national engineering literature. Under Dewart's direction, the department rebuilt several bridges without interrupting traffic. In the mid-1920s, the Department regularly continued bridge construction during the winter months, thereby saving money and speeding completion. In the early 1930s, partly as an economy measure, the department began the practice of repairing and upgrading steel trusses by welding new plates or I-beams, rather than replacing the structure. Under the leadership of Dewart and Melick, Michigan's Highway Department remained at the forefront of innovation in highway bridge design and construction.[34]

Standard steel riveted Parker pony truss bridge (1930), M-65 over the Au Sable River
at Five Channels Dam, Oscoda County. Courtesy of Robert O. Christensen.

M-55 (Mortimer E. Cooley) Bridge (1934) over the Pine River,
Manistee County. Courtesy of Robert O. Christensen.

Standardizing the design of small bridges was a rational, economical approach to a massive problem confronting Michigan's highway engineers in the early twentieth century—how to build enough highways and bridges to keep up with the state's enormous growth of automobile traffic. The State Highway Department engineers did not, however, limit themselves to standardized, short-span bridges. They also completed innovative and aesthetically appealing designs for large bridges as well. The Mortimer E. Cooley (M-55) Bridge (1934) in Manistee County is a notable example of nonstandard design work.

Notes For Chapter 1

1. The best general history of Michigan is Willis F. Dunbar and George May, *Michigan: A History of the Wolverine State,* rev. ed. (Grand Rapids, 1980).

2. For the history of the railroads in Michigan, see Dunbar and May, *Michigan,* pp. 431–444 and Willis F. Dunbar, *All Aboard! A History of Railroads in Michigan* (Grand Rapids, 1969).

3. For the system as it functioned nationally and in Michigan, see George Rogers Taylor, *The Transportation Revolution* (New York, 1951), pp. 15–31, and Philip P. Mason, "The League of American Wheelmen and the Good-Roads Movement, 1880–1905," Ph.D. diss., University of Michigan, 1958, pp. 23–34.

4. Dunbar and May, *Michigan,* p. 568, and Mason, "League of American Wheelmen," p. 220.

5. Richard S. Allen, *Covered Bridges of the Middle West* (Brattleboro, Vt., 1970), pp. 83–86.

6. Alfred P. Boller, *Practical Treatise on the Construction of Iron Highway Bridges, for the Use of Town Committees* (New York, 1876), esp. pp. 90–96.

7. Ibid., pp. 12–13 and C. E. Greene, "Highway Bridges, From the Point of View of the Public," *Michigan Engineer* 8 (1888): 77–78. Precise statistics on bridge failures do not exist and there is considerable disagreement among historians about the extent of the problem. In the 1880s, for example, an average of four to six iron truss railroad bridges failed each year, but highway bridge failures may have been ten times more numerous. For part of the debate, see *Technology and Culture,* 22 (October 1981): 846–850.

8. Donald C. Jackson, "Railroads, Truss Bridges, and the Rise of the Civil Engineer," *Civil Engineering* 47 (1977): 100–101 and Greene, "Highway Bridges," p. 78.

9. J. A. L. Waddell, *The Designing of Ordinary Iron Highway Bridges* (New York, 1884), pp. 157–171.

10. Danko, "Development of the Truss Bridge, 1820–1930, With a Focus Toward Wisconsin," ms. (Madison, Wisconsin, 1976), pp. 30–31; H. K. Vedder, "Highway Bridges in the Manufacturer's Hands," *Michigan Engineer* 13 (1895): 135–142; and Waddell, *The Designing of Ordinary Iron Highway Bridges,* pp. 196–200.

11. Llewellyn N. Edwards, *A Record of the History and Evolution of Early American Bridges* (Orono, Maine, 1959), p. 99, lists the truss types associated with some larger firms.

12. Victor C. Darnell, *Directory of American Bridge-Building Companies, 1840–1900* (Washington, D. C., 1984), *passim.*

13. David H. Miars, *A Century of Bridges: The History of the Champion Bridge Company and the Development of Industrial Manufacturing in Wilmington, Ohio* (Wilmington, Ohio, 1972), *passim,* and Champion Bridge Company Papers, State Archives of Ohio, Columbus, Ohio, *Contract Books, 1884–1942.*

14. David Simmons, "Bridges," ms., p. 10; John Lyle Harrington, ed., *The Principal Professional Papers of J. A. L. Waddell* (New York, 1905), pp. 222–224; and Eli W. Imberman, "The Formative Years of the Chicago Bridge and Iron Company," Ph.D. diss., University of Chicago, 1973, pp. 603–605. Imberman lists sixty-seven midwestern bridge companies engaged in pooling arrangements between 1880 and 1897.

15. Alfred D. Chandler, *The Visible Hand: The Managerial Revolution in American Business* (Cambridge, Mass., 1977), pp. 331–336 and Darnell, *Directory,* pp. 85–86.

16. Dunbar and May, *Michigan*, pp. 714, 745, and John B. Rae, *The American Automobile: A Brief History* (Chicago, 1965), pp. 65–68, 238.

17. Dunbar, *All Aboard!*, pp. 212, 229–246.

18. Ibid., pp. 212, 278.

19. Ibid., pp. 242–243 and Dunbar and May, *Michigan*, pp. 569, 573.

20. Dunbar and May, *Michigan*, pp. 270–279; Philip P. Mason, "League of American Wheelmen," pp. 85–99; and Philip P. Mason, "Horatio S. Earle and the Good-Roads Movement in Michigan," Michigan Academy of Science, Arts, and Letters, *Papers* 43 (l958): 269.

21. For a comprehensive treatment of the Wheelmen, see Mason, "League of American Wheelmen," *passim*; Mason, "Horatio S. Earle," pp. 270–273, 278; and Frank F. Rogers, *History of the Michigan State Highway Department, 1905–1933* (Lansing, l933), pp. 11–13.

22. Mason, "Horatio S. Earle," pp. 273–276 and Rogers, *History*, pp. 14–15.

23. Rogers, *History*, pp. 21–28.

24. Ibid., pp. 63–64.

25. Ibid., pp. 90–94.

26. Dunbar and May, *Michigan*, p. 572 and Bruce E. Seely, *Building the American Highway System: Engineers as Policy Makers* (Philadelphia, 1987), p. 80.

27. Rogers, *History*, pp. 103–104 and Dunbar and May, *Michigan*, p. 572.

28. Rogers, *History*, pp. 168–170; State Highway Commissioner, *Fourteenth Biennial Report* (Lansing, 1932), pp. 11–13; and State Highway Commissioner, *Eighteenth Biennial Report* (Lansing, 1940), pp. 3–4.

29. C. A. Melick, "Record of the Work of Bridge Building by State," *Michigan Roads and Pavements* 19 (November 22, 1922): 12–14 and "Summary of the Work of the Bridge Department," *Michigan Roads and Pavements* 22 (January 1, 1925): 29–30.

30. Melick, "Record of Bridge Building," p. 12; C. V. Dewart, "Standard Pony-Truss Bridges for Michigan Highways," *Engineering News* 76 (November 23, 1916): 990; C. V. Dewart, "Standard Concrete Abutments For Michigan Bridges," *Engineering News* 76 (April 20, 1916): 738–739; "Standard Reinforced Concrete Abutment of Michigan Highway Department," *Engineering and Contracting* 47 (April 25, 1917): 401; and "Standard Bridge Plans of Michigan," *Municipal Journal* 42 (April 5, 1917): 476–477.

31. State of Illinois, Highway Commission, Bulletin Number 9, *Modern Bridges For Illinois Highways* (Springfield, Ill., 1912), pp. 12–13; Clifford Older, "Standard Plans Solve Problems of State Highway Bridge Supervision in Illinois," *Engineering News-Record* 78 (April 5, 1917): 31–34; "Kentucky Road Department Has Standard

Bridges," *Engineering News-Record* 79 (August 9, 1917): 255–256; and Melick, "Record of Bridge Building," p. 12.

32. Bruce E. Seely, "Engineers and Government-Business Cooperation: Highway Standards and the Bureau of Public Roads, 1900–1940," *Business History Review* 58 (Spring 1984): 51–77, and "Highway Engineers as Policy Makers: The Bureau of Public Roads," Ph.D diss., University of Delaware, 1982, p. 334. In his dissertation, Seely devotes considerable space to the ongoing relationship between the Bureau of Public Roads and the Michigan State Highway Department. For standard specifications, see Michigan State Highway Commission, *Standard Road and Bridge Specifications* (Lansing, l926).

33. C. A. Melick, "New Standard Low Truss Bridges for Michigan," *Michigan Roads and Forests*, 16 (April 1920); "Standard Bridge Practice of the Michigan State Highway Department," *Concrete* 23 (1923): 3–10, 69–74; and "Standardizing the Design of Highway Bridges," *Canadian Engineer*, October 2, 1923, p. 371.

34. C. V. Dewart, "Erecting Highway Bridges Under Traffic," *Engineering News*, 76 (October 26, 1916): 798–799; "Winter Construction of Road Bridges in Michigan," *Engineering News-Record* 99 (December 8, 1927): 914–916 and C. A. Melick, "Old Steel Road Bridges Repaired by Welding," *Engineering News-Record* 106 (June 1, 1933): 706–708.

2

American Bridge Designs of the Nineteenth Century and Their Michigan Reflections

There is no reason why a well-designed highway bridge, when properly cared for, should not last forever. Under loads which are light and slowly moving, compared to those of railroad bridges, the iron cannot possibly wear out; and, when properly protected from the weather, it cannot rust. Of course the wooden parts of the structure must be replaced from time to time as they wear out or decay.

J. A. L. WADDELL, in
*The Designing of Ordinary
Iron Highway Bridges,* 1884

In the nineteenth century, highway bridge design underwent significant, but gradual changes. A wide variety of forces brought about changes in bridge design: increased loading requirements; the increased length and difficulty of crossings; shifts in the relative costs of building materials; and the development of new construction materials emerged. The larger railroads, because they required more bridges and much stronger structures than highways, led the way in this field of engineering.[1]

Bridge design evolved gradually so there are no clear-cut chronological watersheds. The earliest bridges were masonry arch structures and combination timber and metal bridges, both popular until about 1870. Railroads began using metal (iron and later steel) trusses in the 1840s, and the metal truss became the dominant design for both railroad and highway bridges from the early 1870s through the 1910s. Steel girder bridges came into common use in the 1890s, initially on railroad lines. Other designs were commonplace as well. Railroads and local governments built timber and metal trestles and viaducts and engineers designed several significant suspension bridges, including one at Newburyport, Massachusetts (1810), well before the Roeblings began their important work. Moreover, iron and steel arch bridges increased in popularity, especially after James B. Eads designed and constructed his path-breaking steel arch railroad bridge crossing the Mississippi River at St. Louis, a novel structure that was completed in 1874. Still, for highway bridges, the masonry arch, wood truss, and the metal truss remained the dominant designs.[2]

The series of bridges built for a single crossing—Michigan Avenue over the Grand River in Lansing—illustrates the evolution of

Timber truss bridge (1856), Michigan Avenue over the Grand River, Lansing. Courtesy of State Archives of Michigan.

American bridge design. The first bridge was a timber structure built in 1848 of unknown design. The second (1856) was a massive uncovered timber Town Lattice through truss, resting on a single pier at midspan. The third structure was a single-span iron bowstring through truss (1871). During a flood of April 1, 1875, which swept away five of Lansing's seven iron bridges, the bowstring truss span at Michigan Avenue survived unscathed, although the River Street bridge passed under it on its way downstream. The Wrought Iron Bridge Company of Canton, Ohio designed and built the fourth bridge at this crossing, a two-span steel-arch design built in 1894 and reputed to have been the widest bridge in the United States, at 116 feet. The city of Lansing moved the bowstring truss a short distance and reinstalled it to carry Kalamazoo Street across the Grand River.[3]

Bowstring arch through truss bridge (1871), Michigan Avenue over the Grand
River, Lansing. Survived a flood in 1875 that destroyed all but two of Lansing's
bridges. Courtesy of State Archives of Michigan.

Steel arch bridge (1894), Michigan Avenue over the Grand River, Lansing. Note
the 1871 span visible through the left arch, in the process of being moved to its
new location at Kalamazoo Street. Courtesy of State Archives of Michigan.

LESLIE HIGH SCHOOL LIBRARY

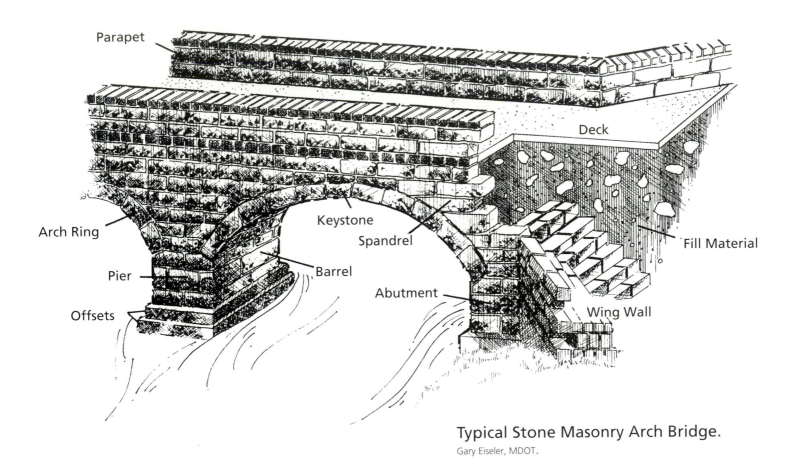

Parapet

Deck

Arch Ring

Keystone

Spandrel

Fill Material

Pier

Barrel

Offsets

Abutment

Wing Wall

Typical Stone Masonry Arch Bridge.

Gary Eiseler, MDOT.

Masonry Arch Bridges

Americans never built masonry arch bridges in large numbers, especially for use as highway bridges. It was an attractive design in terms of strength, durability, low maintenance requirements, and aesthetic appeal.

The enormous amounts of labor needed—especially the skilled labor of stonemasons—made this type of bridge costly. In areas with vast timber resources, such as Michigan, stone arch bridges made little economic sense. Brick masonry construction was even more costly and rare. Well-financed railroads built most stone arch bridges, including spectacular ones in the eastern United States.[4]

East Cass Street bridge. Courtesy of MDOT.

Historic bridges described from this point forward are numbered consecutively and appear on location maps in Appendix A.

1 East Cass Street bridge (1896) over the Kalamazoo River, in downtown Albion, just east of South Superior (M-99), Calhoun County. A rare example of stone arch highway bridge construction. This is also an uncommon three-span structure.

2 South Marshall Avenue bridge (1899) over the Kalamazoo River, just south of downtown Marshall, Calhoun County. One of only two known examples of stone arch highway bridges extant in Michigan.

South Marshall Avenue bridge. Courtesy of MDOT.

White's Bridge, kingpost timber type, Ellsworth, Antrim County. Courtesy of Robert O. Christensen.

Timber Truss Bridges

The timber truss bridge, the forerunner of metal trusses, was the most common type found on roads and railroads through the 1860s. To protect the timbers from weather and reduce rotting, builders often covered the trusses and added wrought iron tension members to strengthen the structure. One simple timber truss form, the kingpost, dates from the Middle Ages. Another, the Burr truss, patented in 1806, combined an arch with the kingpost form. Ithiel Town patented a lattice-web design in 1820, but William Howe developed, and in 1840, patented the most popular wooden truss used in the nineteenth century. Most wooden covered bridges were Howe trusses. Railroads briefly used covered bridges, but they proved inadequate—unable to support the increasing weights of locomotives and cars as well as highly susceptible to fire caused by the sparks from the locomotives.[5]

Today, timber bridges of any type are rare in Michigan. Well into the 1870s, however, communities throughout the state built many covered bridges, including several of noteworthy length. Lansing, Bay City, Saginaw, and above all, Grand Rapids, had large timber truss bridges, including Burr, Howe, and Town lattice types. The first bridge to cross the Grand River at Grand Rapids opened in 1845; the city had three large covered bridges by 1858, at Bridge, Leonard, and Pearl streets. Grand Rapids replaced the original Leonard Street bridge in 1879 with an eight-span 632-foot covered bridge—the longest covered bridge ever built in Michigan.[6]

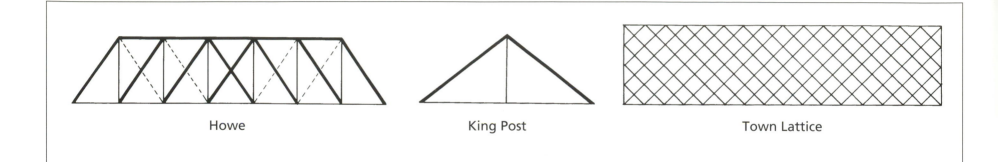

Howe   King Post   Town Lattice

Sheffield Bridge, Three Rivers, St. Joseph County. Timber pony truss with wrought iron diagonals. Courtesy of Robert O. Christensen.

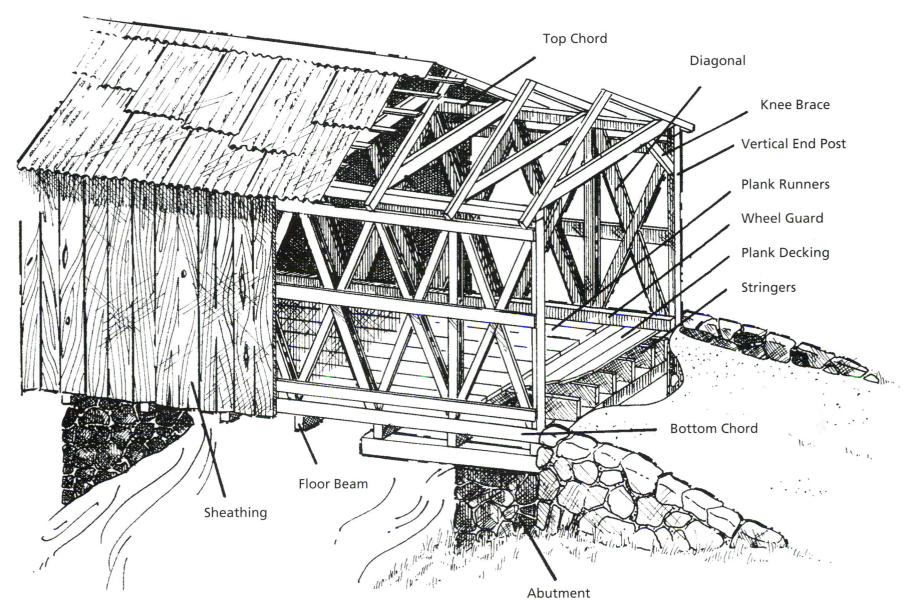

Top Chord

Diagonal

Knee Brace

Vertical End Post

Plank Runners

Wheel Guard

Plank Decking

Stringers

Bottom Chord

Abutment

Floor Beam

Sheathing

Typical Timber Through Truss Covered Bridge.
Gary Eiseler, MDOT.

Leonard Street bridge (1879) over the Grand River, Grand Rapids.
Courtesy of State Archives of Michigan.

White's Bridge. Courtesy of MDOT.

3 White's Bridge (1867), White's Bridge Road over the Flat River, 4 miles southwest of Smyrna, 5.5 miles north of M-21, Ionia County, Through Truss, Timber. This is the oldest surviving covered bridge in Michigan.

Jared N. Bresee and J. N. Walker, two significant timber bridge builders based in western Michigan, built this bridge. White's Bridge uses the Brown Truss, patented by Josiah Brown of Buffalo, New York, in 1857. Like the Howe Truss, the Brown Truss used an "X" arrangement of panel bracing, but had no vertical wrought iron tension members.

57

▲ Fallasburg Bridge. Courtesy of MDOT.

▲ Fallasburg Bridge—detail of Howe Truss showing panel bracing and wrought iron tension member. Courtesy of MDOT.

4 Fallasburg Bridge (1871), Covered Bridge Road over the Flat River, 4 miles northeast of Lowell, Kent County, Through Truss, Timber. This is one of only three surviving covered timber bridges in Michigan. Jared N. Bresee of Ada erected this single-span bridge in 1871 at a cost of $1,500. It is a Howe Truss, 100 feet long, 14 feet wide, and 12 feet high, built of white pine, with 4 by 10 inch floor beams and 4 by 6 inch stringers. The county replaced the original timber abutments with concrete in 1905 and strengthened the timber trusses in 1945 by the addition of steel plates and steel tie rods. A sign over the bridge portal warns the user, "$5 Fine for Riding or Driving On This Bridge Faster Than a Walk."

A trio of iron truss bridges over the Raisin River in Blissfield, Lenawee County. The truss on the right served a railroad, while the other two served local traffic. Courtesy of State Archives of Michigan.

5   Langley Bridge (1887), Covered Bridge Road over the St. Joseph River, 3 miles north of Centreville, St. Joseph County, Through Truss, Timber. A local contractor, Pierce Bodner, of Parkville, was the builder. This is the longest covered bridge in Michigan, with three identical Howe trusses, the most common form used in timber bridges in the nineteenth century. It is a rare three-span timber bridge. Although St. Joseph County inserted steel I-beams under the structure in 1951 for added strength, the Langley Bridge retains its historical integrity

Metal Truss Bridges

The metal truss bridge had great advantages over its timber counterpart. Metal bridges were fireproof and much stronger than timber bridges. They also became comparatively cheaper over the course of the nineteenth century as civilization consumed America's forests, driving up timber prices, while the cost of iron and later steel steadily fell. The first substantial iron truss bridge built in the United States consisted of three Howe trusses with cast iron compression members and wrought iron tension members; it was built in 1845 at Manayunk, Pennsylvania, for the Philadelphia and Reading Railroad. By the early 1850s, railroads used iron truss designs for most of their new bridges.[7]

Large two-span bowstring through truss bridge, over the St. Joseph River
at Niles. Courtesy of Robert O. Christensen.

Two-span Pratt through truss bridge over the St. Joseph River at Niles,
probably a replacement for a bowstring truss at the same location.
Courtesy of Robert O. Christensen.

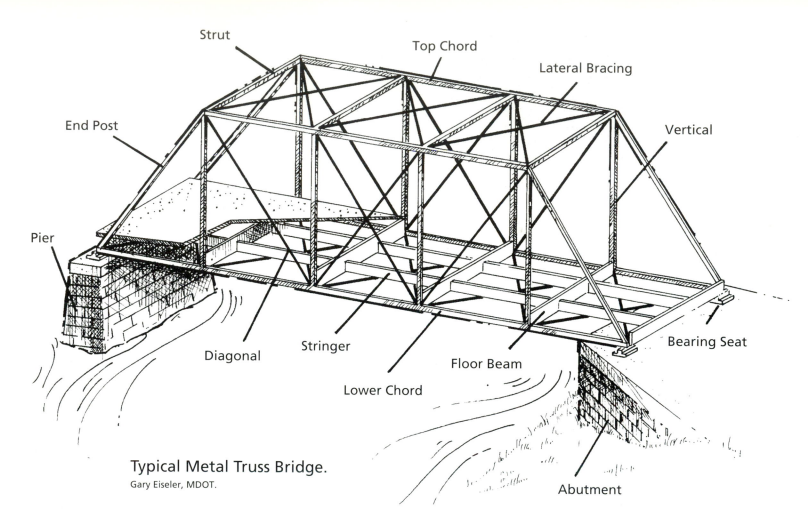

Strut

Top Chord

Lateral Bracing

End Post

Vertical

Pier

Diagonal

Stringer

Lower Chord

Floor Beam

Bearing Seat

Abutment

Typical Metal Truss Bridge.
Gary Eiseler, MDOT.

Several new truss designs emerged as part of the move to metal. Three kinds of metal trusses were the most common in the nineteenth century: the bowstring truss; Thomas and Caleb Pratt's truss, originally wooden, patented in 1844; and the Warren truss, developed and patented in 1848 by British engineers James Warren and Willoughby Monzani. Engineers modified the Pratt in several ways to produce an additional half-dozen truss types: the Whipple or double-intersection Pratt; the Pratt half-hip; the Parker, which is a Pratt with a polygonal top chord; the camelback, a Parker with a top chord of five slopes; and finally, the Kellogg, Baltimore, and Pennsylvania trusses.[8]

The metal truss bridge evolved slowly through the nineteenth and early twentieth centuries. Steel gradually began to replace iron after two successful applications of steel proved its worth: James Eads's 1874 steel arch bridge across the Mississippi and John Roebling's Brooklyn Bridge, a steel suspension bridge opened in 1883. Widespread use of steel began in earnest in the late 1880s, and by the mid-1890s steel had entirely replaced iron in bridge construction. Steel was stronger than iron and became as cheap by the early 1890s, and as iron producers disappeared from the marketplace, bridge fabricators often had no choice but to buy their structural members from the steel mills.[9]

◀ Typical riveted connection, on the HD Road bridge, a deck truss design located in Marquette County. Courtesy of MDOT.

▲ Typical pinned connection, on the 57th Avenue bridge, Allegan County. Courtesy of MDOT.

▶ Ditch Road bridge (1889) over the Shiawassee River, Saginaw County. A rare example of a Thacher truss, but no longer in existence. Courtesy of MDOT.

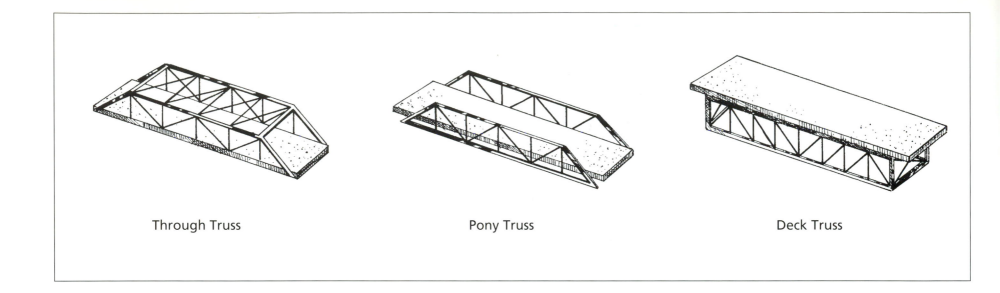

Through Truss   Pony Truss   Deck Truss

Most nineteenth-century American metal trusses used pin connections; that is, the structural members had eyelets at each end and were connected with round pins, allowing the members to rotate around that joint, thus theoretically eliminating bending stress. The use of pinned connections made the erection of the bridge in the field reasonably easy. A disadvantage of pinned connections was the potential lack of rigidity in the truss and its tendency to vibrate. The practice of using turnbuckles to tighten the tension members was only a partial solution. In the mid-1880s, railroads began to use riveted connections on short-span truss and girder bridges, where the riveting could be done in the erection shop and the span shipped already assembled. Still, riveted connections were rare until the development of portable pneumatic riveting machines around 1890, which allowed riveting in the field.[10]

Michigan still has a large number of metal truss bridges, but no examples of the three truss types that were rare in the nineteenth century—the Fink (1850), the Bollman (1851), and the Lenticular truss (1878). Only one example of the bowstring truss remains in the state. Michigan recently lost what was the oldest example of the Thacher truss in the United States, the Ditch Road bridge (1889) over the Shiawassee River in Saginaw County. In 1883, Edwin Thacher developed and patented a hybrid truss incorporating features of the Pratt, Warren, Fink, and Bollman trusses. The Thacher truss was not terribly popular, and fewer than a half dozen still exist nationally.[11]

There are three basic truss types: when the lower chords of the truss carry the traffic deck and lateral supports connect the upper chords, this design is called a through truss;

the same configuration without overhead lateral supports is labeled a pony truss; and when top chords carry the deck, this form is called a deck truss. The remainder of this chapter lists the surviving metal truss bridges in Michigan by type and subtype.

MISCELLANEOUS THROUGH TRUSSES

6 Oakwood Avenue bridge (1876) over the Shiawassee River, in downtown Owosso, Shiawassee County, Through Truss, Double-Intersection Pratt. This is the oldest of only two double-intersection Pratt (Whipple) trusses extant in Michigan. The Wrought Iron Bridge Company of Canton, Ohio, the builder, was one of the most prolific metal truss bridge companies of the midwest during the nineteenth century, with many Michigan bridges to its credit. Along with another bridge of the same age, this is the oldest surviving example in Michigan of the work of the Wrought Iron Bridge Company.

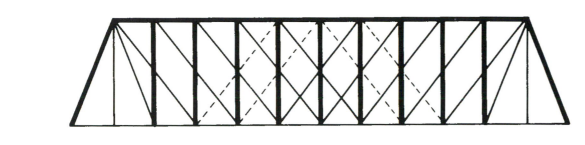

Double Intersection Pratt

Oakwood Avenue bridge. Courtesy of MDOT.

◄ Oakwood Avenue bridge. Detail of double-intersection tension members. Courtesy of MDOT.

▼ Oakwood Avenue bridge. Bridge nameplate. Courtesy of MDOT.

Second Street bridge. Courtesy of MDOT.

Second Street bridge. Courtesy of MDOT.

7 Second Street bridge (1886) over the Kalamazoo River, in the city of Allegan, Allegan County, Through Truss, Double-Intersection Pratt (Whipple). The King Iron Bridge and Manufacturing Company of Cleveland, Ohio, fabricated this single-span bridge in 1886. In 1981, the city of Allegan, by receiving federal approval and funding for its restoration, saved half the cost of replacement. They moved the bridge to dry land, where the construction firm replaced the iron vertical compression members with structural steel members and completed other needed repairs. Following the rehabilitation, which included a new paint job, the contractor returned the bridge to its abutments, and in June 1983, Allegan marked the reopening of this historic bridge with a three-day civic celebration dubbed "Bridgefest," a tradition that continues to this day.

Upton Road bridge. Courtesy of MDOT.

8 Kent Street (Townline) bridge (1907) over the Grand River, just south of Portland and I-96, Ionia County, Through Truss, Parker. This is one of only three Parker through trusses remaining in Michigan. The builder, Wynkoop & McGormley of Toledo, Ohio, was a significant midwestern metal truss bridge firm through the last quarter of the nineteenth century and the early decades of the twentieth century.

9 Turner Road bridge (1910) over the Grand River, 5 miles southeast of Portland, Ionia County, Through Truss, Parker. This bridge, built by Wynkoop & McGormley of Toledo, Ohio, is one of only three Parker through trusses in the state.

10 Upton Road bridge (1901) over the Maple River, 0.5 mile northwest of Elsie, Clinton County, Through Truss, Parker. This is one of only three Parker through trusses found in Michigan. It is the only truss clearly linked to the Detroit Bridge and Iron Works, which built few metal truss bridges in Michigan.

Parker

Upton Road bridge. Courtesy of MDOT.

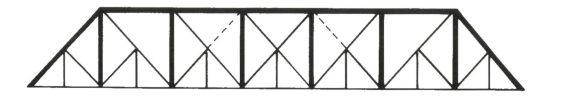

Baltimore

Jones Road bridge. Courtesy of MDOT.

11 Jones Road bridge (1898) over the Grand River, 1.5 miles south of M-21, 4 miles southwest of Fowler, Clinton County, Through Truss, Baltimore. This is the only known Baltimore through truss highway bridge extant in Michigan.

12 Fort Street bridge (1902) over the Power Canal, Sault Ste. Marie, Chippewa County, Through Truss, Pennsylvania. One of only two Pennsylvania through truss highway bridges left in Michigan. This design, common for railroad bridges, was rare for highway bridge applications. The builder, the New Castle Bridge Company of New Castle, Indiana, was a prolific nineteenth century metal truss bridge company.

13 County Road 510 bridge (before 1919) over the Dead River, Negaunee Township, 3 miles north of US-41, Marquette County, Through Truss, Pennsylvania. A rare Pennsylvania through truss highway bridge, particularly because of the length (271 feet) of this single span. The State Highway Department purchased this bridge in 1919, moved it from an unspecified site on the Allegheny River in Pennsylvania, probably considerably upstream from Pittsburgh, and then reerected it on this site in 1921.

Jones Road bridge. Courtesy of MDOT.

Pennsylvania

County Road 510 bridge. Courtesy of MDOT.

Pratt

PRATT THROUGH TRUSSES

14 Maple Road bridge (1876) over the Huron River, 1 mile north of M-14, northwest of Ann Arbor, Washtenaw County, Through Truss, Pratt. One of two metal truss bridges in Michigan dating from 1876, making it one of the two oldest in the state. The builder, the Wrought Iron Bridge Company of Canton, Ohio, was one of the most prolific nineteenth-century metal truss bridge companies in the Midwest, with many Michigan bridges.

15 Tallman Road bridge (1880) over the Looking Glass River, 3 miles west of Wacousta, Clinton County, Through Truss, Pratt. One of the older metal through truss spans in Michigan. Although no nameplate has survived, the bridge's structural details closely resemble bridges built by the Penn Bridge Works of Beaver Falls, Pennsylvania, one of a small number of eastern bridge companies with several bridges in Michigan.

16 Ingalls Road bridge (1884) over the Flat River, just south of Smyrna, Ionia County, Through Truss, Pratt. The Massillon Bridge Company of Massillon, Ohio, was the fourth largest builder of Michigan metal truss bridges, and this is the oldest known surviving example of this company's work in Michigan.

17 East Burt Road (Morseville) bridge (1885) over the Flint River, just west of Morseville, Saginaw County, Through Truss, Pratt. The Smith Bridge Company of Toledo, Ohio, was the fifth most prolific builder of metal truss bridges in Michigan, and this is the oldest surviving example of the firm's work. This bridge has unusual decorative end posts, a distinctive feature of a few metal through trusses of the era.

18 Sixth Street bridge (1886) over the Grand River, Grand Rapids, Kent County, Through Truss, Pratt. The Massillon Bridge Company of Massillon, Ohio, fabricated this bridge, which consists of four Pratt trusses. Originally, all four trusses were 152 feet long, but in 1921, the city of Grand Rapids, after building a concrete retaining wall, shortened the western-most span to 82 feet and made the entire bridge 545 feet long. This is the second oldest surviving through truss built by Massillon in Michigan and the oldest truss bridge of its size remaining in the state. In 1976, following great public protest over plans to demolish this bridge, the city of Grand Rapids reconsidered its decision and in 1979–1980 rehabilitated the structure.

19 Maple Rapids Road bridge (1888) over the Maple River, two miles northwest of Elsie, Clinton County, Through Truss, Pratt. The Variety Ironworks of Cleveland, Ohio, was one of several medium-sized companies that built metal truss bridges throughout the Midwest in the nineteenth century. This is the only known surviving example of this firm's work in Michigan.

▲ Sixth Street bridge. Detail of railing post. Courtesy of MDOT.

◄ Sixth Street bridge. Looking through the trusses. Courtesy of MDOT.

Bridge Street bridge. Courtesy of MDOT.

20 Bridge Street bridge (1890) over the Grand River, city of Portland, Ionia County, Through Truss, Pratt. A rare two-span metal through truss, with two spans 100 feet in length, it features decorative treatment of the end posts. This is the oldest known surviving example of a truss bridge built in Michigan by the Groton Bridge and Manufacturing Company of Groton, New York, a significant eastern bridge manufacturing firm. The city of Portland rehabilitated this bridge just in time to celebrate its centennial.

21 Bell Road bridge (1891) over the Huron River, 1 mile north of Hudson Mills, Washtenaw County, Through Truss, Pratt. Built by the Wrought Iron Bridge Company of Canton, Ohio, the prolific nineteenth-century builder of metal truss bridges in Michigan, this is the third oldest known surviving example of its work in Michigan.

22 Sterling Road bridge (1893) over the St. Joseph River, three miles northwest of Jonesville, Hillsdale County, Through Truss, Pratt. This is an early example of the Michigan work of the Smith Bridge Company of Toledo, Ohio, particularly notable because of the ornamental details on its portal cross bracing.

▲ Bridge Street bridge. Detail of railing. Courtesy of MDOT.

▲ Bridge Street bridge. Looking through the trusses. Courtesy of MDOT.

23 Six Mile Creek Road bridge (1896) over the Shiawassee River, 5 miles north of Owosso, 0.5 mile east of M-52, Shiawassee County, Through Truss, Pratt. The only known surviving example of metal truss bridges built in Michigan by the Morse Bridge Company of Youngstown, Ohio, one of many medium-sized truss bridge companies located in the Midwest in the nineteenth century. It is notable for its distinctive portal and top lateral bracing.

24 Buckner Road bridge (1900) over the St. Joseph River, just south of Mendon, St. Joseph County, Through Truss, Pratt. A late example of a metal truss bridge built in Michigan by the Massillon Bridge Company of Massillon, Ohio, one of the prolific nineteenth-century bridge companies.

25 Alaska Avenue bridge (1905) over the Thornapple River, three miles northeast of Caledonia, Kent County, Through Truss, Pratt. The only known surviving example of a Michigan bridge built by the Attica Bridge Company of Attica, Indiana, a firm established in 1896 and one of dozens of small midwestern bridge firms of that era. This is among the longest single-span metal truss bridges, at 155 feet.

Smith's Crossing bridge. Courtesy of MDOT.

26 22 ½ Mile Road bridge (1906) over the St. Joseph River, two miles west of Homer, Calhoun County, Through Truss, Pratt. The Elkhart Bridge and Iron Company of Elkhart, Indiana, was one of many medium-sized metal truss bridge companies in the Midwest during the late nineteenth and early twentieth centuries. This is the only known surviving example of their work in Michigan.

27 Smith's Crossing bridge (1907) over the Tittabawassee River, near Mapleton, Midland County, Through Truss, Pratt. A large bridge, with two spans of 150 feet each, featuring decorative treatment of the end posts and top portal bracing. No plaque has survived, but the detailing so closely resembles other bridges built by the Joliet Bridge and Iron Company of Joliet, Illinois, it is probably a Joliet design.

WARREN THROUGH TRUSSES

28 Shaytown Road bridge (1913) over the Thornapple River, 2 miles east of Vermontville, Eaton County, Through Truss, Warren. One of only a few Warren through trusses built in Michigan, an unusual example because it is a pin-connected Warren, whereas riveted connections were the rule for Warren trusses of this vintage.

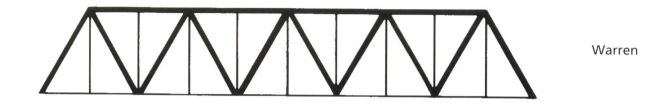

Warren

Smith's Crossing bridge. Courtesy of MDOT.

Truss bedstead bridge over the Cheboyganing River, Saginaw County,
no longer in existence. Courtesy of State Archives of Michigan.

MISCELLANEOUS PONY TRUSSES

The most common type of old bridge left on the highway system is the metal pony truss: more than two hundred survive in Michigan. They are the most difficult type of bridge to evaluate for historical significance, in part because there is little information about their construction dates and builders. Ordinary Pratt pony trusses have survived in large numbers in Michigan, including 129 that were built between 1885 and 1928. These have few noteworthy design features and are not easily distinguished from each other except in terms of size and age. A smaller number of Warren pony trusses, a total of 75 built between 1890 and 1930, have survived.

With few exceptions, Michigan's metal pony trusses are single-span bridges less than 100 feet long. There are some rare surviving examples in Michigan of individual truss types, such as the bowstring or leg bedstead forms.

Bowstring Arch-truss

Elm Circle Drive bridge. Courtesy of MDOT.

29 Elm Circle Drive bridge (1900) over the Lower Rouge River, between John Daly and Inkster roads, north of Michigan Avenue, city of Inkster, Wayne County, Pony Truss, Bowstring Arch. This is the only known surviving example of a bowstring arch truss on a Michigan public road. The builder was the C. J. Glasgow Company of Detroit.

30 Meskill Road bridge (1907) over the Belle River, 3 miles southeast of Memphis, St. Clair County, Pony Truss, Leg Bedstead. A rare surviving examples of truss leg bedstead pony truss bridge in Michigan. This had been a common design for short-span bridges in the 1870s and 1880s, but less common thereafter.

31 Hemlock Road bridge (1912) over the North Branch of the Bad River, 4 miles west of St. Charles, Saginaw County, Pony Truss, Parker. A representative example of a riveted Parker pony truss bridge of medium size (119 feet).

◀ Elm Circle Drive bridge. Courtesy of MDOT.

▼ M-65 bridge. Courtesy of MDOT.

32 M-65 bridge (1930) over the Au Sable River, at the Five Channels Dam, Iosco County, Pony Truss, Parker. This riveted Parker truss bridge has two main spans of 120 feet each, and an total length of 320 feet, making it one of the longest of this type in the state. The State Highway Department designed the structure, and Walter Toebe was the builder. It is an example of a steel pony truss bridge from the end of the steel truss era.

Twenty-One Mile Road bridge. Courtesy of MDOT.

PRATT PONY TRUSSES

33 Twenty-One Mile Road bridge (1885) over Rice Creek, 3 miles northeast of Marshall, Calhoun County, Pony Truss, Pratt. An early Pratt pony truss, built by the Massillon Bridge Company of Massillon, Ohio, a prolific metal truss bridge company constructing bridges in Michigan and the Midwest.

34 Welch Road bridge (1885) over Prairie Creek, 3 miles northeast of Ionia, Ionia County, Pony Truss, Pratt. One of the oldest known surviving metal pony trusses in Michigan. The Penn Bridge Works of Beaver Falls, Pennsylvania, an important eastern bridge company with few Michigan bridges, was the builder.

35 Sorby Highway bridge (1899) over Fitts Creek, 1.5 miles south of Addison, between Manitou and Raymond roads, Lenawee County, Pony Truss, Pratt. A late nineteenth-century metal pony truss built by Smith-Wynkoop and McGormley, contracting agents for the Massillon Bridge Company of Massillon, Ohio.

Big Hill Road bridge. Courtesy of MDOT.

36 Big Hill Road bridge (1905) over the Fawn River, 3 miles southeast of Sturgis, St. Joseph County, Pony Truss, Pratt. With a main span of eighty-four feet, this is among the longest of the known surviving Pratt pony trusses built in Michigan after 1900 because only 10 percent of them exceed eighty feet.

37 Balk Road bridge (1910) over the Fawn River, 4 miles southwest of Sturgis, St. Joseph County, Pony Truss, Pratt. With a main span of eighty-four feet, this is among the longest of the known surviving Pratt pony trusses built in Michigan after 1900.

38 Kelly Road bridge (1920) over the Muskegon River, Butterfield Township, Missaukee County, Pony Truss, Pratt. With a main span of 80 feet, and a total length of 104 feet, this is among the longest surviving Pratt pony trusses built in Michigan after 1900.

WARREN PONY TRUSSES

39 Gorbell Road bridge (1899) over Hog Creek, 6 miles northeast of Coldwater, just east of US-27, Branch County, Pony Truss, Warren. One of four known surviving examples of pony trusses built in Michigan by the Toledo Bridge Company (Smith Bridge Company) before 1900. The Smith-Toledo Bridge Company was one of the most prolific nineteenth century Ohio-based bridge firms.

40 Holy Island Road bridge (1903) over the South Arm of Lake Charlevoix, east of M-66, Charlevoix County, Pony Truss, Warren. This is the only known surviving example of a pony truss bridge built in Michigan by the Wabash Bridge Company of Wabash, Indiana. This bridge firm, which began building bridges in 1896, was one of many small bridge companies that emerged in the Midwest in the 1890s.

41 Armour Saari Road bridge (1906) over the Whitefish River, in Deerton, 2 miles south of M-28, Alger County, Pony Truss, Warren. One of many pony trusses built in Michigan by the Joliet Bridge and Iron Company of Joliet, Illinois, in the early twentieth century.

42 Glassman Road bridge (1908) over the Galien River, 3 miles northeast of New Buffalo, Berrien County, Pony Truss, Warren. This is the only known surviving example of a pony truss bridge built by the Elkhart Bridge and Iron Company of Elkhart, Indiana.

43 Anton Street bridge (1902) over the Sebewaing River, just east of Back Street (M-25), Sebawaing, Huron County, Pony Truss, Warren. With a main span of ninety feet, this is among the longest known surviving Warren pony truss bridges in Michigan.

44 Custer Road bridge (1905) over the Black River, 5 miles south of Deckerville, Sanilac County, Pony Truss, Warren. With a main span of eighty-four feet, this is among the longest known surviving Warren pony truss bridges in Michigan.

45 West Main Street (Eagle River Road) bridge (1909), over the Eagle River, in Eagle River, Keweenaw County, Pony Truss, Warren. The Joliet Bridge and Iron Company of Joliet, Illinois designed and built this pony truss bridge in 1909. This riveted Warren truss span is eighty feet in length, one of the longest of its type in Michigan.

46 West Verne Road bridge (1911) over Misteguay Creek, 3 miles west of Verne, Saginaw County, Pony Truss, Warren. With a main span of eighty feet, this is among the longest known surviving Warren pony truss bridges in Michigan.

47 Rutledge Road bridge (1914) over the Munuscong River, northeast corner of Mackinac County, Pony Truss, Warren. This is the only known surviving example of a pony truss bridge built in Michigan by the Central State Bridge Company of Indianapolis, Indiana. With a main span of eighty-one feet, it is also among the longest known surviving Warren pony truss bridges in Michigan.

HD Road bridge (1935) over the Dead River, Marquette County, no longer in existence, but similar to the US-23 bridge. Courtesy of MDOT.

48 County Road 497 bridge (1917) over the Sturgeon River, 6 miles north of Nahma Junction, Delta County, Pony Truss, Warren. One of several surviving examples of pony truss bridges built by the Joliet Bridge and Iron Company of Joliet, Illinois, the third most prolific builder of metal truss bridges in Michigan. With a main span of 102 feet, it is also among the longest known surviving Warren pony truss bridges in Michigan, where only 15 percent of the total number exceed eighty feet.

49 Downington Road bridge (1920) over the South Branch of the Cass River Drain, 14 miles west of Deckerville, Sanilac County, Pony Truss, Warren. With a main span of ninety feet, this is among the longest known surviving Warren pony truss bridges in Michigan.

DECK TRUSSES

50 US-23 bridge (1937) over the Ocqueoc River, 14 miles northwest of Rogers City, Presque Isle County, Deck Truss, Pratt. One of only two known surviving examples of deck truss highway bridges in Michigan. This is a small (106 feet) riveted Pratt deck truss with massive steel members.

▼ M-26 bridge. Nameplate.
Courtesy of MDOT.

TRUNK LINE BRIDGE
BUILT BY
STATE HIGHWAY DEPARTMENT
FRANK F ROGERS COMMISSIONER
FABRICATED BY
WISCONSIN BRIDGE & IRON CO.
MILWAUKEE WIS.
1915

▲ M-26 bridge. Courtesy of MDOT.

51 M-26 (Lakeshore Drive) bridge (1915) over the Eagle River, in Eagle River, Keweenaw County, Deck Truss, Warren. This riveted steel Warren Deck Truss, with a main span of 105 feet, carried a state trunkline over a deep gorge formed by the Eagle River within the town of Eagle River. The Wisconsin Bridge & Iron Company of Milwaukee, Wisconsin, built the bridge super-structure using plans provided by the Michigan State Highway Department. This was one of the earliest examples of the use of standard bridge designs on state trunklines. The Michigan Department of Transportation recently replaced this bridge with a timber arch bridge, the first of its type on a Michigan state highway, while retaining the historic structure for use as a pedestrian bridge.

Notes For Chapter 2

1. Jackson, "Railroad Truss Bridges," *passim.*

2. The most important general histories of American bridges are David Plowden, *Bridges: The Spans of North America* (New York, 1974); Carl W. Condit, *American Building Art: The Nineteenth Century* (New York, l960), pp. 75–196, 240–254; and Carl W. Condit, *American Building Art: The Twentieth Century* (New York, 1961), pp. 82–150, 195–218.

3. Albert E. Cowles, *Past and Present of the City of Lansing and Ingham County, Michigan* (Lansing, 1905), pp. 70–71.

4. Condit, *The Nineteenth Century*, pp. 240–246, and Plowden, *Bridges*, pp. 9–32.

5. Plowden, *Bridges*, pp. 37–40.

6. Allen, *Covered Bridges of the Middle West,* pp. 88–91.

7. Condit, *The Nineteenth Century*, p. 104.

8. Donald C. Jackson and Barnes Riznic, "Kauai's Opaekaa Bridge: The Only Known British Truss Bridge in the United States," *Industrial Archeology* 13 (Summer 1978): 168; Plowden, *Bridges*, pp. 57–70, 125–140; and Condit, *The Nineteenth Century*, pp. 103–162.

9. Plowden, *Bridges*, pp. 130–138; Waddell, *Bridge Engineering* 1: 28; and Danko, "Development of the Truss Bridge," pp. 19–20.

10. Danko, "Development of the Truss Bridge," pp. 21–23; Waddell, *Bridge Engineering*, 1: 30–31; and Simmons, "Bridges," pp. 11–12.

11. Donald C. Jackson, "The Thacher Truss," Society For Industrial Archeology *Newsletter*, 9 (January/March 1979): 9.

American Bridge Designs of the Twentieth Century and Their Michigan Reflections

Throughout the entire design of this bridge, an effort was made to have it pleasing in appearance without the use of superficial ornamentation and without increasing its cost appreciably. To this end, the general proportions were studied by means of a considerable number of sketches and preliminary drawings.

L. W. MILLARD,
describing the design of the
Mortimer E. Cooley Bridge
(1935) in *Civil Engineering*
(September 1937)

Bridge design changed considerably in the twentieth century. Engineers chose steel trusses for ordinary highway bridge applications less often in the 1910s than before and in only rare instances in the 1920s. Sometimes, steel girders replaced trusses, but the most common highway bridges built between 1900 and 1940 were reinforced concrete arches and girders. Reinforced concrete had many advantages over metal in bridge applications. Stronger, less expensive, and easier to maintain than steel, concrete bridges could be built by small contractors using local labor. Concrete became the most popular construction material for highway bridges of all sizes through the Second World War.

Steel gradually began to replace iron after two successful applications proved its worth—Eads's arched bridge across the Mississippi at St. Louis and Roebling's Brooklyn Bridge. Widespread use of steel began in earnest in the late 1880s, and by the mid-1890s, steel had entirely replaced iron in bridge construction. Steel was stronger than iron and, by the 1890s, became as cheap. As iron manufacturers disappeared from the market, bridge fabricators often had no choice but to buy their structural members from steel producers who became increasingly monopolistic over time.[1]

Steel Girder Bridges

Railroads adopted the metal girder for short spans of less than 100 feet starting in 1847 with a 54 foot deck girder made of boiler plate, thus the origin of the "plate girder" bridge. Not until cheap steel came on the scene in the 1890s did steel plate girder and I-beam bridges come into common use on railroads and highways. In Michigan, forty-nine steel girder spans, built between 1886 and 1939, still exist on the highway system. Of these, only five are through plate girders, and the rest are deck girders of several types.[2]

Marquette Street bridge. Courtesy of MDOT.

52 Marquette Street bridge (1890) over the Penn Central Railroad, 0.75 mile north of M-25, Bay City, Bay County, Steel Girder, Through Plate. This is the oldest of four known surviving through plate girder bridges in Michigan. With a main span of 82 feet and a total length of 152 feet, this is a medium-sized bridge of this type.

53 72nd Avenue bridge (1886) over White Creek, just west of 52nd Street, 3 miles south of I-94, Van Buren County, Steel Girder. Probably the oldest known surviving example of short-span steel girder highway bridges in Michigan, with decorative wrought iron railings.

54 Smith Road bridge (1895) over the Red Cedar River, 0.5 mile southeast of Fowlerville, just south of I-96, Livingston County, Steel Girder. One of the oldest known surviving examples of short-span steel girder bridges in Michigan, with decorative wrought iron railings. The builder was the Beach Manufacturing Company of Charlotte, Michigan, one of only a few bridge companies based in Michigan.

Marquette Street bridge. End of plate girder span. Courtesy of MDOT.

55 Teachout Road bridge (1895) over Wolf Creek, 3 miles southeast of Onsted, Lenawee County, Steel Girder. One of the oldest known surviving examples of short-span steel girder bridges in Michigan, with decorative wrought iron railings.

56 Knight Highway bridge (1899) over Black Creek, 3 miles northwest of Adrian, Lenawee County, Steel Girder. One of the oldest known surviving examples of short-span steel girder bridges in Michigan, with decorative wrought iron railings.

57 Britain Avenue bridge (1900) over Valley Drive, Ox Creek, and the C & O Railroad, city of Benton Harbor, Berrien County, Steel Girder. At 386 feet, this six-span bridge is among the largest 10 percent of known surviving steel girder bridges in Michigan.

Military Street bridge (1857) over the Black River, Port Huron, St. Clair County. This was the second timber swing bridge at this site. Courtesy of the Port Huron *Times-Herald*.

58 East Erie Street bridge (1908) over the South Branch of the Kalamazoo River, 3 miles east of Homer, Calhoun County, Steel Girder. This is an unusual design in that the sidewalks on both sides of the roadway are distinct, separate structures.

59 MacArthur Road bridge (1920) over Lake Creek, just south of Saranac, Ionia County, Steel Girder. An unusual design where the bridge and the superstructure of the concrete dam that it passes over are connected.

60 Beal City Road bridge (1916) over the South Branch of the Salt River, 4 miles northeast of Mt. Pleasant, 3 miles east of US-27, Isabella County, Steel Girder. The builder of this bridge was the U.S. Steel and Culvert Company of Bay City, Michigan, one of only a small number of Michigan-based steel bridge companies. It also features decorative wrought iron railings.

Moveable Bridges

There are three major types of moveable bridges. The swing span is a specialized truss type that pivots ninety degrees on a center pier. In a vertical lift bridge machinery raises the entire span at both ends simultaneously. On a bascule bridge, one end of the span or leaf rises, while the other end, usually fitted with counterweights, falls. The swing bridge was the most common moveable bridge type built during the nineteenth and early twentieth centuries.

Initially, all three moveable bridge types (swing, vertical lift, and bascule) were of tim-

Military Street bridge (1884) over the Black River, Port Huron, St. Clair County. An iron truss swing span that replaced the 1857 bridge and remained in use until 1913. Courtesy of the Port Huron *Times-Herald*.

ber construction. One of the earliest iron truss swing bridges—perhaps the first in the United States—was built in 1856 to carry Rush Street over the Chicago River. From 1903 until 1923, the largest bridge fabricator in the United States, the American Bridge Company, built 316 moveable bridges, including 232 swing spans, nearly three-quarters of the total, 68 bascule spans, and 16 vertical lift bridges.[3]

Michigan showed a similar preference for swing spans. According to a list of bridge crossing navigable waters prepared by the U.S. Army Corps of Engineers in 1925, Michigan's 57 moveable bridges included 44 swing spans, 12 bascule bridges, and one vertical lift bridge. Of the bascule spans, all built after 1912, 8 crossed the Rouge River below Ford's River Rouge factory complex.[4]

SWING BRIDGES

61 57th Street bridge (1900) over the Kalamazoo River, 2 miles north of Fennville, Allegan County, Pony Truss, Warren and Swing Spans. The Kalamazoo River was navigable from Lake Michigan well inland until the late 1920s. This bridge, which consists of six spans and measures 429 feet in length, had a hand-operated swing span that was still in service as late as 1925.

Typical small metal truss swing bridge, Manistee, Michigan, date unknown.
Courtesy of State Archives of Michigan.

62 Grosse Ile Bridge Road (Grosse Ile Toll) Bridge (1913) over the Trenton Channel, north end of channel, Wayne County, Through Truss, Camelback and Swing. This bridge consists of four camelback through truss spans and a camelback swing span. With a total length of 995 feet, this is one of the longest metal truss bridges in the state.

63 Grosse Ile Parkway bridge (1931) over the Trenton Channel, middle part of the channel, Wayne County, Camelback Through Truss (Swing) and Girder. This bridge has ten steel girder spans, each 118 feet long, and a single camelback through truss swing span 340 feet in length, yielding a total length of 1350 feet. The

Augustus J. Dupuis Company of Detroit built this structure for the Michigan Central Railroad. This was the last through truss swing bridge constructed in Michigan.

Large swing span carrying U.S.-31 over the Grand River, in Grand Haven,
no longer in existence. Courtesy of Robert O. Christensen.

◄ 57th Street bridge. The postcard caption simply calls this a "wagon bridge." Courtesy of Robert O. Christensen.

▼ 57th Street bridge. The manually–turned swing span. Courtesy of MDOT.

Grosse Ile Toll bridge. Courtesy of MDOT.

Grosse Ile Parkway bridge. Photograph by Charles K. Hyde, 1975.

▲ Military Street bridge. Detail, rack and pinion gears, center girder of north leaf. Photograph by Carla Anderson, 1990.

◄ Military Street bridge (1914–1991) over the Black River, Port Huron, St. Clair County, no longer in existence. Photograph by Carla Anderson, 1990.

BASCULE BRIDGES

The modern bascule bridge was a product of the late nineteenth century, when manufacturers developed powerful electric motors and engineers improved the techniques for counterbalancing the weight of the moveable span. Bascule bridges were superior to swing bridges for narrow channels and in congested areas. Chicago was the birthplace of the two basic bascule bridge designs, the rolling lift (1893) and the "Chicago Type" trunnion style (1900). Bascule highway bridges, whether employing the rolling lift or trunnion design, normally have two spans or leafs and use deck trusses or girders. Michigan has only five surviving examples of bascule bridges built before 1941 for highways, all of them double-leaf.[5]

▲ US-31 bridge. This bridge is also named the American Legion Memorial Bridge. Courtesy of Robert O. Christensen.

▲ US-31 bridge. Operator's control house. Courtesy of MDOT.

64 Fort Street (Old US-25) bridge (1926) over the Rouge River, 0.25 mile northwest of the I-75 bridge over the Rouge River, Wayne County, Bascule. This is one of the oldest of a set of a dozen bascule bridges built on the Rouge River in the 1920s to allow shippers to use the river for access to the Ford Motor Company River Rouge manufacturing complex. The Chicago Bascule Bridge Company was the builder.

65 Dix Avenue bridge (1926) over the Rouge River, Detroit, Wayne County, Bascule. The Wisconsin Bridge and Iron Company built this double-leaf bascule bridge. It is one of a dozen moveable bridges across the Rouge River between the Detroit River and the Ford Motor Company River Rouge manufacturing complex.

66 West Jefferson Avenue bridge (1922) over the Rouge River, in southwestern Detroit, at the Detroit-River Rouge border, Wayne County, Bascule. The Missouri Valley Bridge and Iron Company built this double-leaf bascule bridge. Following a major rehabilitation project in 1981–1982, when MDOT replaced the original machinery, this bridge has returned to service.

US-41 (Houghton-Hancock) bridge. Courtesy of MDOT.

67 Second Avenue bridge (1939) over the Thunder Bay River, city of Alpena, Alpena County, Bascule. Winner of the American Institute of Steel Construction Annual Award of Merit, this bascule bridge was designated the Most Beautiful Steel Bridge in 1939. The general contractor was the W. J. Storen Company, the R. C. Mahan Company erected the structural steel, and the Hall Electric Company completed the electrical work.

68 US-31 bridge (1933) over the Manistee River, city of Manistee, Manistee County, Bascule, Scherzer Type. The Scherzer Rolling Lift Bridge Company designed this bridge, and the Strom Construction Company served as the general contractor.

VERTICAL LIFT BRIDGES

69 US-41 (Houghton/Hancock) bridge (1959) over Portage Lake, Houghton County, Vertical Lift. A monumental double-deck, vertical lift bridge, the only one of its type in Michigan. It features a lower deck carrying railroad lines and an upper deck with four lanes for highway traffic. Overall, it is 1,310 feet long, with a lift span 260 feet long. The State Highway Department engineered this structure, which cost more than $13 million. The two railroads that used the bridge shared in the costs of construction. The Al Johnson Construction Company was the general contractor, while the American Bridge Company had the steel contract.

M-28 bridge. Courtesy of MDOT.

Other Steel Bridges

Nationally, steel remained the preferred material for bridges of monumental size in the early twentieth century. The steel arch form was a common design for large bridges in the metropolitan New York City area during the 1910s, but this design is rare in Michigan; the M-28 bridge (1930) over the Ontonagon River and the Ashmun Street bridge (1934) in Sault Ste. Marie are the two oldest examples. The International Bridge (1962), also in Sault Ste. Marie, has two

large steel arches, along with several deck truss spans. The largest steel truss bridges built in the United States were cantilever trusses. The Blue Water Bridge (1938) is an outstanding example of this type. The Mortimer Cooley Bridge (1935) in Manistee County and the Cut River Bridge (1946) in Mackinac County, are excellent examples of steel cantilever designs on a smaller scale. Michigan's two suspension bridges, the Ambassador Bridge (1929) and the Mackinac Straits Bridge (1958), are both outstanding examples of suspension bridge design and

important engineering achievements in their own right.[6]

STEEL ARCHES

70 M-28 bridge (1930) over the Middle Branch of the Ontonagon River, 4 miles west of Trout Creek, Ontonagon County, Steel Arch, Deck. This is one of only three steel arch bridges in Michigan, with the main arch span 150 feet in length. The State Highway Department designed this bridge, which the firm of Meads and Anderson built.

M-28 bridge, above; detail of metal railing, right.
Both photos courtesy of MDOT.

Ashmun Street bridge. Courtesy of Robert O. Christensen.

71 Ashmun Street bridge (1934) over the Power Canal, Sault Ste. Marie, Chippewa County, Steel Arch, Through. One of only three steel arch bridges in Michigan, this massive structure measures 42 feet in width and 257 feet in length. The Michigan State Highway Department designed the structure and Fry & Kain, Inc. and Robert Hudson were the builders. While the new bridge was under construction, the old bridge was left standing and used as falsework to support the new structure.

72 Interstate 75 (International) Bridge (1962) over the St. Mary's River, Chippewa County, Steel Arch, Through. One of Michigan's five monumental bridges, with five main through arch spans, two of 540 feet each, one of 430 feet, and two smaller spans of 200 feet each. With its lengthy approaches, the bridge is more than two miles long. The main spans had to be built without obstructing traffic through the navigation locks. The contractor achieved this result through the balanced addition of steel structural members on the main spans until they met.

Ashmun Street bridge. Courtesy of MDOT.

International Bridge. Courtesy of MDOT.

CANTILEVERED STEEL TRUSSES

73 M-55 (Mortimer E. Cooley) Bridge (1935) over the Pine River, 21 miles east of Manistee, Manistee County, Deck Truss, Cantilevered. The State Highway Department designed this bridge, named in honor of Mortimer E. Cooley, dean of the College of Engineering at the University of Michigan from 1904 to 1928. The Cooley Bridge, with its total length of 555 feet, is notable on aesthetic grounds as well; it won the American Institute of Steel Construction Award for the most beautiful structure in its class built during 1935.

74 US-2 bridge (1946) over the Cut River, 4 miles west of Brevort, Mackinac County, Deck Truss, Cantilevered. One of only two cantilevered deck truss bridges in Michigan, it is 641 feet long and contains 888 tons of structural steel. The State Highway Department designed this structure, and W. J. Meager and Sons, Contractors, built it.

Two views of M-55 (Mortimer E. Cooley) Bridge. Above, courtesy of
Robert O. Christensen. Below, courtesy of MDOT.

◀ US-2 bridge. Courtesy of MDOT.

▼ Interstate 69, 94 (Blue Water)
Bridge. Courtesy of MDOT.

Ambassador Bridge. View from Canadian side of the Detroit River. Courtesy of MDOT.

75 Interstate 69, 94 (Blue Water) Bridge (1938) over the St. Clair River, St. Clair County, Through Truss, Cantilevered. The state of Michigan and the province of Ontario jointly built this bridge linking Port Huron, Michigan, and Sarnia, Ontario, at a cost of $4 million. The structure has a main span of 871 feet with a pair of anchor arms, each 326 feet long, and produces a clearance of 152 feet above the river.

STEEL SUSPENSION

76 Ambassador Bridge (1929) over the Detroit River, Wayne County, Suspension. One of only two suspension bridges built in Michigan, this opened to traffic as the longest suspension bridge in the world, extending a total of 9,602 feet with approaches. The main span is 1,850 feet long. The chief engineer was Jonathan Jones from the McClintic-Marshall Company of Pittsburgh, the prime contractor. The construction of this bridge involved several significant achievements, including the replacement of all the wire cables after McClintock-Marshall had strung them and had already suspended the stiffening trusses.

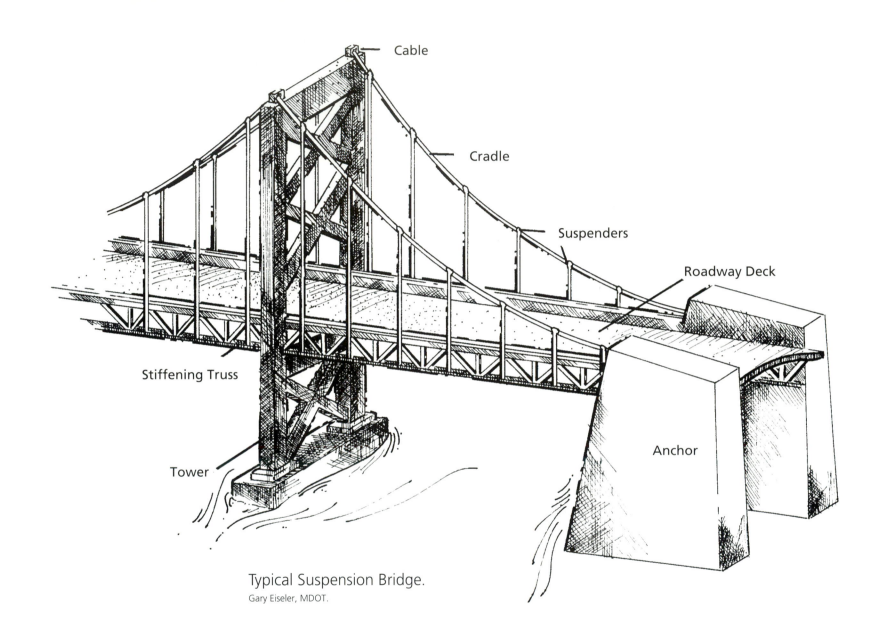

Cable

Cradle

Suspenders

Roadway Deck

Stiffening Truss

Tower

Anchor

Typical Suspension Bridge.
Gary Eiseler, MDOT.

110

Interstate 75 (Mackinac Straits) Bridge. Courtesy of MDOT.

77 Interstate 75 (Mackinac Straits) Bridge (1958) over the Straits of Mackinac, Emmet and Mackinac counties. This is one of only two suspension bridges built in Michigan. It is one of the monumental suspension bridges of the world, with an total length of 17,918 feet, a center span of 3,800 feet, two side spans of 1,800 feet, and two backstay spans of 472 feet, giving it a total length of 8,614 feet between anchorages, the longest in the world at the time of completion. David B. Steinman designed the bridge for the Mackinac Bridge Authority. The American Bridge Division of the United States Steel Corporation won the steel superstructure contract, while the substructure contract went to the Merritt-Chapman and Scott Corporation of New York City. C. E. Haltenhoff served as the project engineer, while Steinman retained G. B. Woodruff as a consulting engineer. This engineering monument opened to traffic on November 1, 1957, with all work completed in September 1958.

Washington Avenue bridge over the Grand River, Lansing, no longer
in existence. Courtesy of State Archives of Michigan.

Reinforced Concrete Bridges

Engineers first developed reinforced concrete
bridge designs in France and Switzerland in
the early 1880s. Ernest Ransome designed
the first American concrete arch, built in San
Francisco in 1889. American engineers,
along with Europeans working in the United
States, experimented with several systems of
reinforcing in the 1890s, including the use of
wire mesh, iron bars, and steel I-beams. By
the turn of the century, Ransome's system of
reinforcing with iron rods and bars became
the most popular system for bridges.[7]

A few monumental arched railroad and
highway bridges used reinforced concrete
designs through the 1930s. More important,
however, was the popularity of reinforced
concrete for ordinary highway bridges of all
sizes. Concrete bridges had many advantages
over steel trusses, including strength, low initial cost, and low maintenance requirements.
Small contractors using local materials and
labor could build them, thus, the buyer was
free from the near-monopoly grip of the steel
bridge industry.[8]

Maple River bridge, Muir, Ionia County, no longer in existence.
Courtesy of Robert O. Christensen.

Plainwell bridge over the Kalamazoo River, Plainwell, Allegan County,
no longer in existence. Courtesy of Donald C. Jackson.

The use of concrete designs also brought a return to the more local, decentralized patterns of bridge design and construction that had existed before the coming of the metal truss in the 1870s. The State Highway Department developed standard designs for concrete girder bridges, but city engineers or Michigan-based engineering firms usually designed concrete arch bridges and did not use standard designs. The Illinois Bridge Company, based in Chicago, was a rare example of an out-of-state bridge company that built a substantial number of concrete bridges in Michigan. In its 1914 catalogue of concrete bridges, one-third of the twenty-one examples the company used of its work were Michigan bridges.[9]

The highway commissioner provided detailed information on contracts involving 162 concrete bridges either completed or underway in Michigan by July 1920. Forty-eight firms built these bridges, but only three companies accounted for more than four structures each. The largest, the Illinois Bridge Company, built eleven, followed by E. C. Nolan & Son from Detroit with nine bridges, and the Hicks Construction Company from Iron Mountain with seven.[10]

Observers on timber truss bridge over the Grand River at Grand Ledge,
Ingham County, watching pile driving for the piers of a new reinforced
concrete arch bridge. Courtesy of Robert O. Christensen.

Concrete Arch bridge (1910) over the Grand River, Grand Ledge, Ingham
County, no longer in existence. Note piers of the old timber truss bridge
through center span. Courtesy of Robert O. Christensen.

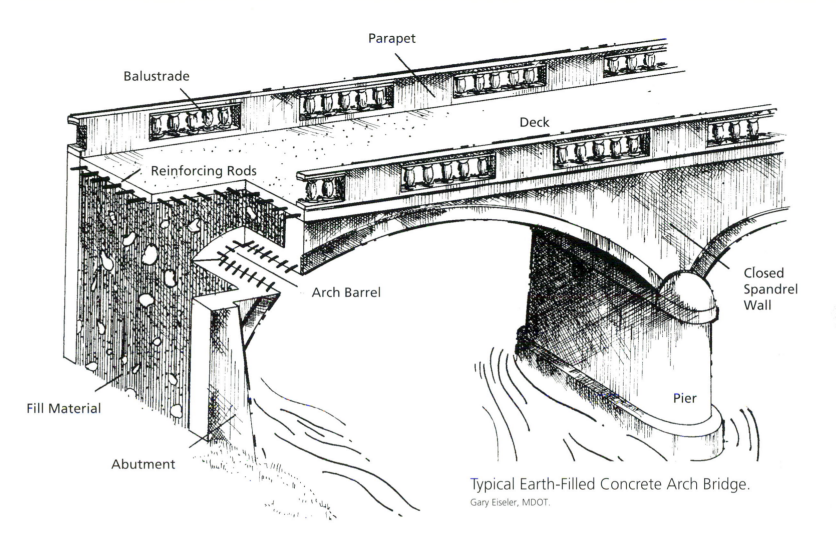

Typical Earth-Filled Concrete Arch Bridge.
Gary Eiseler, MDOT.

EARTH-FILLED CONCRETE ARCHES

78 Front Street bridge (1902) over the Boardman River, in downtown Traverse City, Grand Traverse County, Concrete Arch, Earth-Filled. This is a rare early example of a reinforced concrete bridge built before 1905. It is typical of the patterns of bridge construction that emerged with the coming of reinforced concrete: a small local firm, the Monroe Construction Company of Charlevoix, Michigan, was the contractor.

79 West Michigan Avenue bridge (1903) over the Battle Creek River, in downtown Battle Creek, Calhoun County, Concrete Arch, Earth-Filled. A rare early example of a reinforced concrete bridge built before 1905.

80 McCamly Street bridge (1904) over the Battle Creek River, in downtown Battle Creek, Calhoun County, Concrete Arch, Earth-Filled. One of only four known surviving examples of reinforced concrete bridges built in Michigan before 1905.

Twelve Mile Road bridge. Courtesy of MDOT.

81 Twelve Mile Road bridge (1907) over the St. Joseph River, east of Burlington and south of M-60, Calhoun County, Concrete Arch, Earth-Filled. An early example of concrete arch construction and the earliest known surviving example built by the Illinois Bridge Company of Chicago, the only out-of-state firm to build a large number of concrete bridges in Michigan.

82 Michigan Railway Engineering Company (Interurban Walk) bridge (1915) over the Grand River, in downtown Grand Rapids, Kent County, Concrete Arch, Earth-Filled. At a length of 472 feet, this is the third longest surviving earth-filled concrete arch bridge in Michigan. The Fargo Engineering Company of Kalamazoo, Michigan, a major Michigan civil engineering firm in the early twentieth century and the corporate predecessor of Commonwealth Associates, designed this bridge for the Michigan Railway Engineering Company, which used it initially to carry its street railway lines across the Grand River. It now serves as a pedestrian bridge.

M-3 bridge. Courtesy of Donald C. Jackson.

M-3 bridge. Courtesy of MDOT.

▲ Elizabeth Park Drive bridge. Courtesy of MDOT.

◀ Elizabeth Park Drive bridge. Decorative obelisk on parapet. Courtesy of MDOT.

83 M-3, Southbound, bridge (1920) over the Clinton River, in Mt. Clemens, Macomb County, Concrete Arch, Earth-Filled. This is the fifth longest earth-filled concrete arch bridge known to survive in Michigan, with a total length of 241 feet.

84 Elizabeth Park Drive bridge (1923) over the Elizabeth Park Canal, in the city of Trenton, Wayne County, Concrete Arch, Earth-Filled. A. W. Kutche and Company, Contractors, built this bridge in a park setting. It features decorative elements, including concrete obelisks on top of the parapet.

121

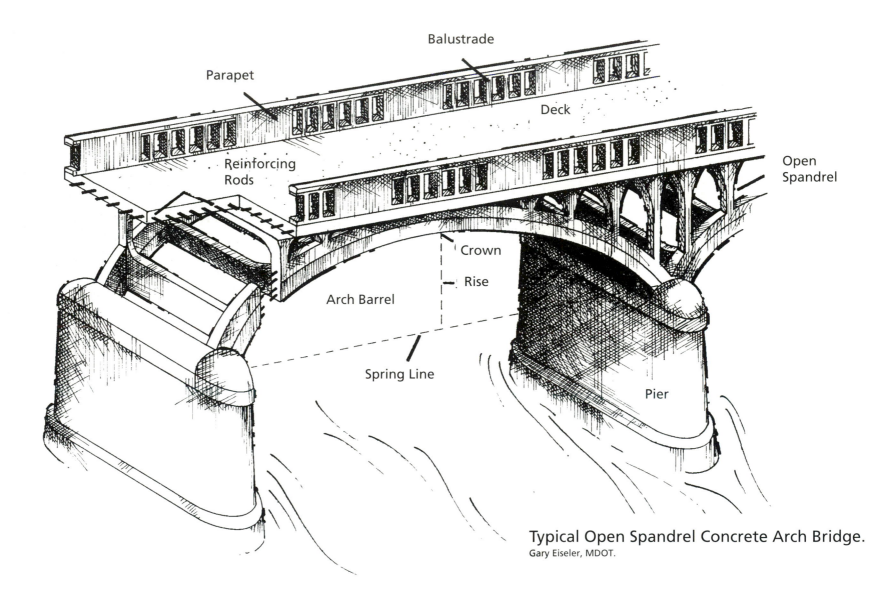

Parapet

Balustrade

Deck

Reinforcing Rods

Open Spandrel

Crown

Rise

Arch Barrel

Spring Line

Pier

Typical Open Spandrel Concrete Arch Bridge.
Gary Eiseler, MDOT.

Belle Isle (General MacArthur) Bridge. Courtesy of MDOT.

OPEN SPANDREL CONCRETE ARCHES

85 Belle Isle (General MacArthur) Bridge (1923), foot of East Grand Boulevard in Detroit, over the Detroit River to Belle Isle, Wayne County, Concrete Arch, Open Spandrel. This monumental structure consists of nineteen spans, with a total length of 2,356 feet. It features cantilevered arches, allegedly only the second example of a bridge of this type in the United States when it opened. The city of Detroit completed a major rehabilitation of this bridge in 1984–1985,

at a cost of $11.4 million. The project included repairs to the arches, an entirely new deck and road surface, and the installation of "New Jersey barriers" between the roadway and the sidewalks.

86 M-69 bridge (1924) over the Paint River, just east of Crystal Falls, Iron County, Concrete Arch, Open Spandrel. The Michigan State Highway Department designed this two-span bridge and the firm of Smith-Holmes-Burridge-

Sparks built it. The bridge features attractive decorative lamp posts and railings.

87 M-45 (Fulton Street) bridge (1928) over the Grand River, downtown Grand Rapids, Kent County, Concrete Arch, Open Spandrel. This five-span bridge is the second longest example of an open spandrel design known to survive in Michigan, with a total length of 536 feet.

Belle Isle (General MacArthur) Bridge. Arch ribs after
rehabilitation in 1984–1985. Courtesy of MDOT.

M-45 (Fulton Street) bridge. Courtesy of MDOT.

M-45 (Fulton Street) bridge. Detail showing arch ribs and spandrels. Courtesy of MDOT.

Pine Island Drive bridge. Courtesy of MDOT.

THROUGH CONCRETE ARCHES

88 Pine Island Drive bridge (1924) Over the Rogue (*sic*) River, just north of 10 Mile Road, Kent County, Concrete Arch, Through. One of only two concrete through arch bridges known to survive in Michigan, it features concrete top bracing. This bridge type, often called the rainbow arch, was common in other midwestern states, but not in Michigan.

89 Merrick Street bridge (1926) over the Raisin River, City of Adrian, 0.63 mile west of Main Street (M-52) and north of Beecher Road (M-34), Lenawee County, Concrete Arch, Through. Jack Lemon, city engineer for Adrian, designed this bridge, one of only two concrete through arch bridges known to survive in Michigan.

Pine Island Drive bridge. Courtesy of MDOT.

Merrick Street bridge. Courtesy of MDOT.

Merrick Street bridge. Courtesy of MDOT.

▲ Ottawa Street bridge. Courtesy of MDOT.

▼ Ottawa Street bridge. Detail of railing pilasters. Courtesy of MDOT.

CONCRETE GIRDERS

◢90◣ Ottawa Street bridge (1900) over the Muskegon River, just west of the south approach to the M-120 Causeway, at the east end of Muskegon Lake, Muskegon County, Concrete Girder. The oldest known surviving example of a concrete girder bridge in Michigan.

◢91◣ County Road I-39 bridge (1916) over the Rapid River, 7 miles north of Rapid River, Delta County, Concrete Girder. This is the oldest known surviving example of a concrete girder bridge designed by the Michigan State Highway Department for the state trunkline system. The Delta Contracting Company of Escanaba, Michigan, was the builder.

Banat to Amberg Road bridge. Courtesy of MDOT.

92 190th Avenue bridge (1916) over the Little Muskegon River, 1 mile southwest of Morley, Mecosta County, Concrete Girder. This is the oldest example of a concrete girder bridge designed by the Michigan State Highway Department. The builder was E. W. Baldwin of St. Louis, Michigan.

93 US-2 ("Siphon") Bridge (1919) over the Manistique River, in Manistique, Schoolcraft County, Concrete Girder. This eight- span girder bridge is 294 feet long overall and is an integral part of a concrete raceway flume. Because the water level in the flume is above the level of the roadway, the bridge acts as a siphon.

94 Banat to Amberg Road (Chalk Hill) bridge (1927) over the Menominee River, 5 miles west of Banat, Menominee County, Concrete Girder, T-Beam. A six-span concrete T-Beam bridge, the fifth longest concrete girder bridges in the state, with a total length of 327 feet. The firm of Sioems, Helmers, & Schaffer, from St. Paul, Minnesota, was the contractor. This bridge features decorative concrete railings with attractive light standards.

Banat to Amberg Road bridge. Detail of light standard.
Courtesy of MDOT.

95 West Mitchell Street (US-31) bridge (1930) over the Bear River, city of Petoskey, Emmet County, Concrete Girder. This is the fourth longest concrete girder bridge in Michigan, with seven spans providing a total length of 330 feet. The Michigan State Highway Department designed the bridge, and the Whitney Brothers, Contractors, built the structure. It has several decorative features, including railings and piers.

West Mitchell Street (US-31) bridge. Courtesy of MDOT.

West Mitchell Street (US-31) bridge. Courtesy of MDOT.

CONCRETE CAMELBACKS

96 Old M-28 bridge (1920) over the Rock River, Baraga County, 3 miles east of Covington, Concrete Girder, Camelback. This is the oldest known surviving example of a standard Michigan State Highway Department concrete camelback bridge of 60 feet. In the late 1910s, Michigan's Highway Department was a national leader in developing standard designs as a way of producing inexpensive bridges for the state trunkline system.

97 Portsmouth Road bridge (1921) over Cheboyganing Drain, two miles north of M-81, northeast of Saginaw, Saginaw County, Concrete Girder, Camelback. This is the oldest known surviving example of a standard Michigan State Highway Department concrete camelback bridge of 70 feet. L. A. Davison & Company was the contractor for this bridge.

98 County Road 569 bridge (1923) over the Sturgeon River, three miles east of Foster City, Dickinson County, Concrete Girder, Camelback. This is the oldest known surviving example of a standard Michigan State Highway Department concrete camelback bridge of seventy-five feet. David Graham of Minnesota was the contractor for this bridge.

US-12 (Mottville) bridge. Courtesy of MDOT.

99 Grange Road bridge (1916) over Stony Creek, 2 miles south of M-21 and 3 miles southwest of Fowler, Clinton County, Concrete Girder, Camelback. This is the oldest known surviving example of a standard Michigan State Highway Department concrete camelback bridge of ninety feet. The contractor for this bridge was Price Brothers of Lansing.

100 Okemos Road, Northbound, bridge (1924) over the Red Cedar River, downtown Okemos, Ingham County, Concrete Girder, Camelback. One of only two known surviving examples of concrete girder camelback bridges in Michigan with sidewalks built as an integral part of the original structure. Because the State Highway Department built most camelback bridges in rural areas, it seldom included sidewalks in the design.

101 US-12 (Mottville) Bridge (1922) over the St. Joseph River, in Mottville, St. Joseph County, Concrete Girder, Camelback. This three-span bridge, with a total length of 270 feet, is the longest known surviving example of a concrete camelback bridge designed by the Michigan State Highway Department. It consists of three standard ninety-foot spans. The contractor was the firm of Smith & Nichols of Hastings, Michigan. This bridge now serves pedestrians and bicyclists only, while vehicular traffic uses a new replacement structure located nearby.

US-12 (Mottville) bridge. Courtesy of MDOT.

102 M-32 Spur bridge (1922) over the Thunder Bay River, 9 miles east of Atlanta, Montmorency County, Concrete Girder, Camelback. This two-span bridge, with a total length of 150 feet, is the third longest known surviving example of a concrete camelback bridge designed by the Michigan State Highway Department. It consists of two standard seventy-five-foot spans.

103 East Michigan Avenue bridge (1923) over the Kalamazoo River, just east of Galesburg, Kalamazoo County, Concrete Girder, Camelback. This three-span bridge, with a total length of 210 feet, is the second longest known surviving example of a concrete camelback bridge designed by the Michigan State Highway Department. The East Michigan Avenue Bridge consists of a center span of ninety feet and two side spans of sixty feet, all standard State Highway Department design. William Marshall and Son of Grand Rapids, Michigan, was the builder.

104 Genesee Road bridge (1925) over the Grand Trunk Western Railroad, in Lapeer, Lapeer County, Concrete Girder, Camelback. This three-span bridge, with a total length of 147 feet, is the fourth longest known surviving example of a concrete camelback bridge designed by the Michigan State Highway Department. It has a center span of sixty-seven feet and two side spans of forty feet each.

M-32 Spur bridge. Courtesy of Robert O. Christensen.

Grand River Avenue bridge (1925) over the Grand Trunk Western Railroad,
Novi, Oakland County, no longer in existence. Identical to the Genessee Road
Bridge (1925). Photograph by Carla Anderson, 1991.

Grand River Avenue bridge (1925), Novi, Oakland County.
Construction photograph showing the pouring of concrete.
Courtesy of State Archives of Michigan.

Notes For Chapter 3

1. Plowden, *Bridges*, pp. 130–138; Waddell, *Bridge Engineering* 1: 28; and Danko, "Development of the Truss Bridge," pp. 19–20.

2. Condit, *Nineteenth Century*, pp. 106–107. Waddell, *Bridge Engineering* 1: 408–412, discussed the advantages of steel girder designs over trusses.

3. Otis Ellis Hovey, *Moveable Bridges* (New York, 1926), 1: 12–15, 28.

4. U.S. Department of War, U.S. Army, Corps of Engineers, *List of Bridges Over the Navigable Waters of the United States, 1925* (Washington, D.C., 1926), p. 324.

5. Plowden, *Bridges*, pp. 186–188 and Hovey, *Movable Bridges* 1: 89–110.

6. Condit, *Twentieth Century*, pp. 104–150, and Plowden, *Bridges*, pp. 171–181.

7. Condit, *Nineteenth Century*, pp. 247–254.

8. Plowden, *Bridges*, pp. 297–319 and Condit, *Twentieth Century*, pp. 195–207. For a discussion of analytical and aesthetics problems faced by engineers in using reinforced concrete, see David P. Billington, "History and Esthetics in Concrete Arch Bridges," American Society of Civil Engineers, *Journal of the Structural Division* 103 (November 1977): 2129–2143.

9. Illinois Bridge Company, *Bridges of Concrete and What They Cost* (Chicago, 1914).

10. Michigan State Highway Commission, *Eighth Biennial Report* (Lansing, 1920), pp. 32–41.

CHAPTER

Bridge Design and Construction in Michigan Since World War II

Michigan's highway system, including its bridges, has changed substantially since the Second World War in response to a large growth in motor vehicle traffic. While state population grew by nearly 50 percent between 1945 and 1990 (6.3 million to 9.2 million), the number of vehicles nearly tripled (2.5 million to 7.0 million), and the total miles traveled increased more than sixfold, from 12 billion to 78 billion miles per year. Michigan built about 11,000 miles of new highways during those years, including more than 1,000 miles of interstate highways following the passage of the Interstate Highway Act of 1956. About 3,000 of the 4,500 bridges now on state trunklines (Interstates, US-routes, and M-routes) were built since 1945.

The state highway commissioner's *Biennial Reports* from 1945 through 1958 reveal much about the focus of bridge construction in the postwar years. Although some federal aid funds went to local units of government for local bridge projects, the bulk of moneys went for replacing bridges on the existing trunklines, for new bridges on re-aligned segments of trunkline highways, and for expressway construction in Detroit. The State Highway Department gradually extended the Edsel Ford Expressway, begun during the war as the Detroit Industrial Expressway linking Dearborn with Ypsilanti, into Detroit starting in 1947. Work on the John C. Lodge Expressway began in the late 1940s. During the 1948–1950 biennium, Michigan spent nearly half of its $11.6 million in federal aid for bridges on these two expressways. The Interstate Highway Act later more than doubled spending on bridge work, from $40 million in 1955–1956 to $72 million in 1957–1958, and created a severe shortage of engineers within the State Highway Department. Rather than risk losing federal aid, the State Highway Department relied heavily on outside consultants to complete design work for bridge projects.

Interstate 75 (Rouge River) Bridge. Construction of concrete
piers, viewed from across the Rouge River, July 1965.
Courtesy of MDOT.

Interstate 75 (Rouge River) bridge. Artist's rendition of the bridge, early 1965. Courtesy of MDOT.

105 Interstate 75 (Rouge River) bridge (1966) over the Rouge River, Detroit, Wayne County. This monumental structure carries Interstate 75 over the Rouge River and allows this highway to come into Detroit from the south. Built at a cost of $21 million, this steel girder structure has 115 spans, is nearly 8,400 feet in length, and provides an underclearance of 100 feet for ships. It is the largest bridge designed by the State Highway Department and is one of four monumental bridges along the 395–mile Interstate 75 extending from the Ohio border to Sault Ste. Marie.

Bridge engineers with the State Highway Department relied on a few well-tested designs in the late 1940s. They normally used reinforced concrete T-beams for spans less than forty feet and steel I-beam designs for longer spans. Because of severe shortages of steel during the Korean War, bridge engineers tried to use concrete as much as possible, even if this meant increasing the number of spans to reduce their length. They also used cantilevered or continuous steel beam designs to economize on the use of steel. Concrete arch and steel truss designs virtually disappeared in the postwar years.

In addition to many small and mid-sized bridges of standard design constructed on the state trunkline system, the State Highway Department and its descendant, the Michigan Department of Transportation (MDOT), built Michigan's most notable monumental bridges. The most important of these, discussed in chapter 5, were the Mackinac Straits Bridge (1958), the Houghton-Hancock Vertical Lift Bridge (1959), the International Bridge (1962) linking the twin cities of Saulte Ste. Marie in Michigan and Ontario, and the Zilwaukee Bridge (1988) over the Saginaw River. Additionally, the Rouge River Bridge (1966), which carried Interstate 75 over the Rouge River, should be noted. The largest bridge designed by the State Highway Department, this steel girder structure of 115 spans is nearly 8,400 feet long.

The Michigan State Highway Department introduced several important innovations in bridge design in the postwar period. Highway department engineers experimented with air-entrained concrete on bridges and grade separations to reduce the impact of road salt on these structures. Incorporating air bubbles into the concrete combats the effects of road salt, which causes spalling (splitting) of the surface concrete, allowing water to seep into the bridge members. The freeze-thaw cycle leads to severe cracking, by enabling the salt to attack the steel reinforcing rods, eventually resulting in irreversible deterioration. Air-entrainment became standard practice by 1948.

In the early 1960s, the highway department dropped the traditional practice of riveting steel bridge members and adopted on-site welding instead, saving erection costs in the process. The department also experimented in the late 1960s with "weathering" steel in bridge design. Weathering steel oxidized to the point of producing a protective coating that then prevented further oxidizing and therefore reduced maintenance costs by reducing the need to paint. The experiment had mixed results, in large part because the road salt used on the state's highways and bridges altered the behavior of the steel. Finally, the Michigan Department of Transportation (MDOT) began experiments in the late 1980s to protect bridge decks from corrosion by installing cathodes to carry low-voltage electric current through the deck structure.

CHAPTER **5**

Michigan's Big Bridges, From Ambassador to Zilwaukee

The prospect ahead is cause for rejoicing. A bridge such as the one projected will be a logical extension of the system of spans joining nation to nation that at present is composed of the bridges at Montreal, Fort Erie and Niagara. At no place along the border is such a connecting link needed more than it is needed here. At no point can one be more useful or more used.

Editorial, "A Bridge at Last," published in the *Detroit Free Press* on March 11, 1927 referring to announced plans to build the Ambassador Bridge

Michigan's fundamental geographical features are its two peninsulas created by four of the Great Lakes; the lakes in turn, are interconnected by wide rivers and the Straits of Mackinac. In addition, Michigan has a significant system of rivers that end at the Great Lakes. Although water resources have served as important arteries for lake and river transportation throughout Michigan's history, they were also great barriers to long distance travel by road or rail. The railroads initially crossed these broad waters with car ferries. The Grand Trunk Western Railroad opened a tunnel under the St. Clair River between Port Huron and Sarnia, Ontario, in 1891, and in 1909, the Michigan Central Railroad completed a similar project under the Detroit River, linking Detroit with Windsor, Ontario. The last major underwater connection was the Detroit-Windsor Vehicular Tunnel, finished in 1930. With completion of the Ambassador Bridge

(1929) over the Detroit River, the monumental steel structure proved the most economical way to overcome these barriers.

Ambassador Bridge

During the second half of the nineteenth century, the Detroit River became a major bottleneck for railroad traffic to the east coast of the United States via the Great Western Railway, which ran through the Province of Ontario into New York State at Niagara Falls. Originally, the railroads unloaded freight and passengers from their cars on one side of the Detroit River, transferred the goods onto ferries and then moved everything back into railroad cars on the other side. In the late 1860s the development of specialized ferries that carried the railroad cars intact reduced this burdensome transfer, but congestion on both sides of the river worsened in the 1870s; sometimes as many as one thousand cars backed up on each side. Ice jams often closed the river to traffic for weeks at a time.

The initial impetus for a permanent Detroit River crossing came from the railroads. In 1871, James F. Joy began an effort to drive a tunnel under the river, but with its failure, he developed several proposals for a railroad bridge. Following hearings in 1873, the U.S. Army Board of Inquiry rejected out of hand most of the various proposals for bridges using draw or swing spans. The railroad companies and other promoters developed more than a dozen bridge proposals over the next three decades, but the adamant opposition of the powerful Lake Carriers Association plus serious misgivings by the Board—now the Army Corps of Engineers—led to their rejection. The completion of the Michigan Central Railroad's Detroit River Tunnel in 1910 ended agitation for a railroad bridge.

In 1920, Charles Evan Fowler, a prominent New York bridge engineer, proposed a suspension bridge to carry a highway, electric street car lines, and railroad lines across the Detroit River, to begin at 21st Street in Detroit, the alignment ultimately used for the Ambassador Bridge. Fowler formed the American Transit Company and the Canadian Transit Company in 1921 to build the bridge jointly, but he had to withdraw from the project after failing to raise even a small part of the required $15 million by the end of 1922. In April 1924, James W. Austin, an early supporter of Fowler and a major investor in the failed effort, convinced Joseph A. Bower, a New York financier, to support the project. Bower decided to revive plans to build a bridge, but he limited the effort to a single-deck highway bridge, with no provisions for railroads or streetcars. After a long, unsuccessful effort to convince Essex County, Ontario, to provide a subsidy or guarantee for the bridge, Bower decided in March 1927 to build it with private funds. Groundbreaking took place in Detroit on May 7, 1927.

Bower founded the Detroit International Bridge Company, which built the structure and has operated it to this day. They hired the McClintick-Marshall Company of Pittsburgh, a well-established steel fabrication firm, to serve as the general contractor. Jonathan Jones, McClintick-Marshall's chief engineer, designed the bridge and supervised its erection. McClintick-Marshall completed the structure for $11.5 million, with the entire effort, including real estate purchases and a buyout of the predecessor transit companies, at a cost of $22.5 million. After considering several possible names for the bridge, Bower decided in April 1928 to call it the Ambassador Bridge because he thought of the bridge as an ambassador between the two countries.

Construction proceeded rapidly, and by the summer of 1928, McClintick-Marshall had finished the tower piers, the two main towers, and the anchorages. They raised cables to carry footbridges across the bridge on August 8, 1928, and began the major task of stringing 206 individual wires into cable strands, with 37 of these cable strands com-

Ambassador Bridge under construction, September, 1929.
Courtesy of State Archives of Michigan.

prising the suspension cable. McClintick-Marshall's design used galvanized, heat-treated wire, instead of the traditional cold-drawn wire. They completed the cables by December 27, 1928, and hoped to finish the entire project by July 1929.

McClintick-Marshall ordered all work on the Ambassador Bridge stopped on March 5, 1929, following the discovery of a major problem of wire breakage on the Mount Hope Bridge across Narraganset Bay in Rhode Island, a McClintick-Marshall project

using heat-treated cable wire. Following the recommendation of David Steinman, McClintick-Marshall decided to replace the existing cable with cold-drawn wire. This required the dismantling of the main span, which they did by lowering the floor beams and stiffening trusses onto barges in the Detroit River. After removing the old cables and restringing new ones, McClintick-Marshall rebuilt most of the main span in September 1929. Despite this setback, which cost the contractor $1 million, the Detroit

International Bridge Company dedicated the Ambassador Bridge on November 11, 1929, and officially opened it to traffic four days later.

The dedication ceremonies, commencing shortly after three on a cold, grey afternoon, were impressive and memorable. Crowds of about 100,000 on the American side and 50,000 on the Canadian side heard speeches from various officials, including Governor Fred Green of Michigan. Before the formal ribbon-cutting ceremonies could take place

149

at the terminals, however, the crowds broke through the barriers and rushed to the center of the bridge. There, a substantial steel fence and a large police force prevented both crowds from crossing the international boundary. Hundreds from the unruly throng climbed onto the catwalks that ran alongside the main suspension cables and dangled dangerously from various perches on the catwalks all the way up to the top of the towers. At twilight, the large, enthusiastic crowds finally moved off the newly dedicated bridge.

When completed, the Ambassador Bridge had the longest main span (1,850 feet) of any suspension bridge in the world, a distinction it held only briefly, until the George Washington Bridge, with a main span of 3,500 feet, opened in 1931. The two steel towers, which support the main span to provide clearance of 152 feet above the Detroit River, are 363 feet high. The Ambassador Bridge is 3,650 feet long from anchorage to anchorage, and with its lengthy approaches from both the Canadian and American sides, 7,490 feet long overall, measured from abutment to abutment.

Blue Water Bridge. Courtesy of MDOT.

Blue Water Bridge. Courtesy of State Archives of Michigan.

The Ambassador Bridge did not open at a very auspicious time. The New York stock market crash that touched off the Great Depression was only two weeks away and the opening of the Detroit-Windsor Vehicular Tunnel in 1930 provided unwelcome competition. The Detroit International Bridge Company struggled throughout the Second World War before achieving financial stability in the postwar era. The Ambassador Bridge now carries about the same total volume of traffic as the Detroit-Windsor Tunnel, but the bridge supports the lion's share of truck traffic.

Blue Water Bridge

The state of Michigan and the Province of Ontario jointly built this bridge linking Port Huron, Michigan, with Sarnia, Ontario, at a cost of $4 million. The American engineering firm of Modjeski and Masters, with their Canadian partners, the firm of Monsarrat and Pratley, designed the bridge project. The American Bridge Company built the main span, the Wisconsin Bridge and Iron Company completed the American approach spans, while the Sarnia Bridge Company built the Canadian approach spans. The Blue Water Bridge features a steel cantilever design, with a main span 871 feet long and a pair of anchor arms each 326 feet long, providing a clearance of 152 feet above the heavily traveled St. Clair River. The American approach spans (2,283 feet long) and the Canadian approaches (2,657 feet long), a combination of steel deck girder and deck truss spans, give the bridge a total length of 6,463 feet.

The completion of most of Interstate 69 across Michigan in the 1980s and the free trade agreement with Canada has produced considerable new traffic in recent years. Crossings jumped sharply from 3.8 million in 1987 to 6 million in 1990, pushing against the capacity of this three-lane bridge. A major reconstruction of the toll and customs plaza on the American side began in 1991 and discussions are underway about building a new bridge south of the existing span by the end of the decade.

Houghton-Hancock Bridge

This vertical lift bridge is the third span across Portage Lake linking the cities of Houghton and Hancock. The first was a timber swing bridge (1875), while the second was a steel swing bridge that opened in 1905. The state of Michigan completed the present bridge in 1959 at a cost of $13 million. Martin McGrath served as chief engineer for the entire project, while George Jacobson was bridge engineer. The Al Johnson Construction Company was the general contractor. The American Bridge Company built the superstructure, and the Bethlehem Steel Company provided the structural steel.

Houghton-Hancock bridge. Aerial view of construction, with the old swing bridge (1905) clearly visible. Courtesy of Michigan Technological University Archives and Copper Country Historical Collections.

Houghton-Hancock bridge. Water-level view of construction, with lift span
on a barge on the left. Courtesy of Michigan Technological University
Archives and Copper Country Historical Collections.

Houghton-Hancock bridge. Courtesy of MDOT.

Houghton-Hancock bridge. Vertical lift span in the intermediate position.
Courtesy of MDOT.

International Bridge. Construction of concrete piers between the main spans.
Courtesy of State Archives of Michigan.

International Bridge. Aerial view from Sault Ste. Marie, Ontario, looking southwest.
Courtesy of State Archives of Michigan.

The Houghton-Hancock Bridge is a double-deck structure, with a four-lane roadway on the upper deck and railroad tracks on the lower deck. The bridge has a total length of 1,310 feet, with a lift span 268 feet long, supported by twin steel towers 180 feet tall. When trains use the bridge, it remains in its lowest position, and highway traffic uses the automobile level. When the railroads are not using the bridge, the operator leaves the structure in an intermediate position, with vehicular traffic using the railroad deck, allowing small boats to pass underneath. For the passage of large ships, the main span can be raised to provide clearance of 104 feet. Portage Lake is part of the Keweenaw Waterway, which bisects the Keweenaw Peninsula and offers Great Lakes vessels a sheltered passage from storms, especially the gales of November.

International Bridge

A railroad bridge linked the twin cities of Sault Ste. Marie in Michigan and Ontario in 1887, but ferries carried automobile traffic over the St. Mary's River, which divided the two cities until this bridge opened in 1962. The government of Ontario and the Michigan state legislature created the International Bridge Authority in 1935 to plan and finance a highway bridge, but nearly one-quarter of a century passed before construction began. The New York engineering firm of Steinman, Boyton, Gronquist, and London designed this structure, which cost $20 million.

This was an ambitious project because the bridge crossed two navigation canals, one on each side of the international boundary, and the St. Mary's River. The main segment, which rests on sixty-two concrete piers, is 9,280 long, the American approach is 2,471 feet in length, and the Canadian approach spans are 2,942 feet long; thus, the two-lane bridge is nearly three miles long. The most impressive part of the structure is the four-span cantilevered truss, some 1,260 feet long, over the American canal. To avoid interrupting ship traffic, the contractor built the main truss segment without falsework through the balanced addition of steel members as work progressed. The Canadian crossing has a simpler truss span 830 feet long. The entire bridge required 114,000 tons of concrete and 11,000 tons of structural steel for completion.

Mackinac Straits Bridge

The five-mile stretch of water separating Michigan's two peninsulas, the result of glacial action some twelve thousand years ago, has long served as a major barrier to the movement of people and goods. The three railroads that reached the Straits of Mackinac in the early 1880s, the Michigan Central and the Grand Rapids & Indiana Railway from the south, and the Detroit, Mackinac and Marquette from the north, jointly established the Mackinac Transportation Company in 1881 to operate a railroad car ferry service across the straits. The railroads and their shipping lines developed Mackinac Island into a major vacation destination in the 1880s, an effort that culminated with opening the Grand Hotel on the island in 1887. One of the hotel's directors, Commodore Cornelius Vanderbilt, observed on July 1, 1888: "What this area needs is a bridge across the Straits."

Improved highways along the eastern shores of Michigan's lower peninsula brought increased automobile traffic to the straits region starting in the 1910s. The state of Michigan initiated an automobile ferry service between St. Ignace and Mackinaw City in 1923 and eventually operated eight ferry boats. In peak travel periods, particularly during deer season, five mile backups and delays of four hours or longer became common at the state docks at Mackinaw City and St. Ignace.

With increased public pressure to break this bottleneck, the Michigan legislature, with Governor William A. Comstock's approval, established a Mackinac Straits Bridge Authority in 1934, with the power to issue bonds for bridge construction. Prentiss M. Brown served as the authority's legal counsel. The bridge authority supported a proposal first developed

in 1921 by Charles Evan Fowler, the bridge engineer who had previously promoted a Detroit-Windsor bridge. Fowler's plans called for an island-hopping route from the city of Cheboygan to Bois Blanc, Round, and Mackinac islands, thence to St. Ignace, along a twenty-four-mile route. The bridge authority requested loans and grants from the federal Public Works Administration (PWA) in August 1934 for the project, which the PWA flatly rejected eleven months later.

The Mackinac Bridge Authority then hired Francis C. McMath and James E. Cissell to draw up a plan for a direct crossing from Mackinaw City to St. Ignace and submitted this to the PWA in September 1935. Chase Osborne, a former Michigan governor, asked President Franklin D. Roosevelt to support a Mackinac bridge. Roosevelt requested the Army Corps of Engineers study the idea and the Army Corps reported that a bridge was technically and economically feasible. The PWA nevertheless rejected the bridge authority's request for funding.

In 1938, the bridge authority engaged

Fred Masters of the prominent engineering firm of Modjeski and Masters to develop a new design proposal. Masters hired Leon S. Moisseiff, who in 1940 submitted a plan for a suspension bridge with a main span of 4,600 feet. This was simply a larger version of Moisseiff's ill-fated Tacoma Narrows Bridge in Washington State, a structure destroyed by high winds on November 7, 1940. Although that disaster delayed any further action, the activities of 1938–1940 nevertheless produced some important results. The bridge authority conducted a series of soundings and borings across the straits and built a causeway extending out 4,200 feet from the St. Ignace shore. The Second World War ended any additional work, and the Legislature abolished the bridge authority in 1947.

William Stewart Woodfill, president of the Grand Hotel on Mackinac Island, almost singlehandedly resuscitated the dream of a bridge across the Straits of Mackinac. Woodfill formed the statewide Mackinac Bridge Citizens Committee in 1949 to lobby for a new bridge authority, which the legislature

Mackinac Straits Bridge. Temporary catwalks in place, early in the 1956 construction season, before the stringing of the main suspension cables. Courtesy of State Archives of Michigan.

created in 1950. Governor G. Mennen ("Soapy") Williams appointed State Senator Prentiss M. Brown as chairman of the new Mackinac Bridge Authority. A panel of three prominent engineers—Othmar H. Ammann, David B. Steinman, and Glenn B. Woodruff—conducted a feasibility study and made recommendations to the bridge authority on the location, structure, and design of the bridge. The State Highway Department, which had just placed a $4.5 million ferryboat, *Vacationland*, into service at the straits in January 1952, remained hostile to the bridge plan. In April 1952, the Michigan legislature authorized the bridge authority to issue bonds for the project, choose an engineer, and proceed with construction. The authority selected David B. Steinman as the chief engineer in January 1953 and tried unsuccessfully to sell the bridge bonds in April 1953, but by the end of the year, the authority had sold the $99.8 million in revenue bonds needed to begin construction.

Mackinac Straits Bridge. Attaching the suspended span to the suspender
cables, hanging from the main cables, early in the 1957 construction season.
Courtesy of State Archives of Michigan.

Mackinac Straits Bridge. From left to right, the massive concrete anchorage,
backstay span, side span, and main suspended span.
Courtesy of State Archives of Michigan.

Mackinac Straits Bridge. Photograph of nearly completed bridge, May 21, 1958.
Courtesy of State Archives of Michigan.

Besides selecting Steinman, the bridge authority awarded two major contracts—one to the Merritt-Chapman and Scott Corporation of New York for all substructure work, in the amount of $25.7 million, while the second contract went to the American Bridge Division of the U.S. Steel Corporation for the steel superstructure, in the amount of $44.5 million. During construction, Grover C. Denny served as project manager for substructure work, and C. E. Haltenhoff was the project engineer. Steinman retained Glenn Woodruff as a special consulting engineer and J. W. Kinney as his resident engineer.

The major construction achievement of 1954 was the erection of the bridge's six principal piers, including those for the two towers, the anchorages, and the backstay spans. Merritt-Chapman sank enormous steel caissons into the mud under the straits and then drove them to bedrock. After removing all the mud and loose rock, Merritt-Chapman poured the enormous reinforced-concrete piers, which extended to bedrock, more than 200 feet below the water

surface. In 1955, Merritt-Chapman built the remaining twenty-eight piers and completed the anchorage, while American Bridge built the two main towers and installed the backstay spans. The Mackinac Bridge began to take shape in 1956, when American Bridge strung the main cables and built the twenty-eight truss spans that made up the approaches.

The four-year construction effort ended in 1957, with the erection of the main suspension span and paving of the roadway. The new bridge opened to traffic on November 1, 1957, although the contractors did not complete all the work until September 1958. The official bridge dedication ceremonies began on June 25, 1958, when Governor Williams completed the first "Governor's Walk" across the bridge, and ended four days later. The faith and hard work of men such as Prentiss M. Brown, G. Mennen Williams, and David Steinman finally produced results.

The annual Mackinac Bridge Walk began as a walking race sanctioned by the International Walkers Association. The first walk, in June 1958, involved only sixty walkers including Governor Williams. Later bridge

walks took place on Labor Day and the number of participants increased rapidly from about 2,500 in 1962 to more than 15,000 in 1966–1968. After Williams's walk, the next governor to participate was George Romney in 1966. Since then, the bridge walk has become a mandatory political event for governors and gubernatorial candidates. In 1970, more than 20,000 completed the walk and the numbers reached 70,000 in 1990. The Mackinac Bridge Walk is as much an integral part of Labor Day in Michigan as parades and picnics.

The sheer size and beauty of the Mackinac Straits Bridge still impress first-time viewers—a main suspension span of 3,800 feet, two sidespans of 1,800 feet, and two backstay spans of 472 feet each, giving the bridge a total length between anchorages of 8,614 feet, the longest in the world. The total length of the steel superstructure is 19,205 feet, while the total length of the bridge, with approaches, is 26,444 feet, slightly more than five miles. The towers stand 552 feet above the water line, and the bridge provides 155 feet of clearance at

Zilwaukee Bridge, under construction in 1987, looking north, up the Saginaw River. The new bridge dwarfs the older bascule bridge (1960) in the foreground. Courtesy of MDOT.

midspan. Each of the two main cables, with 348 galvanized steel wires, is 25.25 inches in diameter and consists of 37 strands. The main cables contain 12,580 miles of wire, with a total weight of 11,840 tons.

Zilwaukee Bridge

This structure replaced a four-lane double-leaf bascule bridge (drawbridge) completed in 1960 to carry Interstate 75 over the Saginaw River. From its opening day the Zilwaukee drawbridge caused serious prob-

lems for traffic on both I-75 and the Saginaw River. The drawbridge provided a narrow channel of only 150 feet at a point where the Saginaw River turns sharply, creating a significant hazard to navigation. Over the years, several ships have struck the bridge or its protective pilings and occasionally forced the closing of I-75. To make matters worse, ship traffic on the Saginaw River increased four-fold in the 1960s and early 1970s. The more serious problem was the disruption of traffic on I-75 every time the bridge opened. Since

its original construction, traffic greatly exceeded projections; thus, this problem became severe, especially on holiday weekends, when four-hour delays at the bridge were not uncommon. One of only two drawbridges on the entire interstate highway system, it was the worst bottleneck and hazard on the entire 1,800 miles of Interstate 75.

The Michigan Department of Transportation decided to build a replacement high-level bridge just north of the draw-bridge, a decision approved by the Federal

Zilwaukee Bridge, under construction in 1987. This view, looking east, illustrates the length and height of the approaches to the new span.
Courtesy of MDOT.

Highway Administration in 1974. MDOT allowed contractors to submit bids on two different designs for a new bridge, one using standard steel plate girders and the other using a precast segmental concrete design. In August 1979, MDOT accepted a proposal jointly submitted by Stevin Construction of the Netherlands and Walter Toebe Construction Company of Wixom, Michigan for a precast concrete structure. Their bid of $76.8 million was nearly $10 million below the low bid for a steel structure. The new bridge is really two bridges side by side, each with four traffic lanes and shoulders, with the entire structure about 1.5 miles long, providing a clearance of 125 feet over the Saginaw River shipping channel. Construction began in October 1979.

The Zilwaukee Bridge is a post-tensioned, segmental, box girder bridge, with each concrete segment precast in a casting plant at the construction site. The 1,592 concrete segments are either eight feet or twelve feet long, weigh between 120 and 160 tons each, and rest on fifty-two massive concrete pillars. The contractor placed a balanced group of four segments atop each pillar (pier) by using a massive

steel launching girder equipped with a crane; then he pulled them together with steel cables (tendons) several inches thick, which he then stressed (stretched) with hydraulic jacks and locked into place. The builder added two additional segments, one at each end of the span, and then tied these into the other segments with steel tendons as before. The contractor repeated this process until he completed the bridge, using 4,000 miles of post-tensioned steel cables.

Beginning at the north end of the northbound bridge, Stevin Construction began building the bridge segments in 1981. The Walter Toebe Construction Company had completed all fifty-two pillars, and Stevin had half of the twenty-five spans on the northbound bridge finished by late August 1982, when a major accident took place. Overloading crushed temporary compression blocks in an expansion joint on one span and a 300-foot section of the bridge sagged five feet at one end and rose more than three feet at the other end. The most important of many problems created by the accident was damage to the top and footings of one pier. After exhaustive

analysis involving outside consultants, MDOT decided to reconstruct the pier footings and then return the tilted deck section to its intended position. Toebe Construction began repairs in early summer of 1983, completing the work in late March 1984 at a cost of about $7 million.

MDOT reached a negotiated termination of its original contract with Stevin/Toebe, avoiding expensive litigation and allowing the project to proceed quickly. In total, the state of Michigan made payments of $75 million to Stevin/Toebe for their work, including a final settlement of $13 million for the purchase of their equipment and fabrication plant. MDOT then took bids in September 1984 for the completion of the bridge. S. J. Groves & Sons of Minneapolis won the contract with a bid of $35.9 million. The new contractor finished the bridge without any major problems. The northbound bridge opened in December 1987 and the southbound segment in September 1988. The final cost was $123 million, with an additional $10 million for ramps and approaches, and the federal government paid 90 percent of the total cost.

Appendix A

Regional Maps Showing Bridge Locations

1 East Cass Street, over the Kalamazoo River, in downtown Albion, just east of South Superior (M-99), Calhoun County

2 South Marshall Avenue, over the Kalamazoo River, just south of downtown Marshall, Calhoun County

3 White's Bridge Road, over the Flat River, 4 miles southwest of Smyrna, 5.5 miles north of M-91, Ionia County

4 Covered Bridge Road (Fallasburg Bridge) over the Flat River, 4 miles northeast of Lowell, Kent County

5 Covered Bridge Road (Langley Bridge) over the St. Joseph River, 3 miles north of Centreville, St. Joseph County

6 Oakwood Avenue, over the Shiawassee River, in downtown Owosso, Shiawassee County

7 Second Street, over the Kalamazoo River, City of Allegan, Allegan County

8 Kent Street (Townline Bridge), over the Grand River, just south of Portland and I-96, Ionia County

9 Turner Road, over the Grand River, 5 miles southeast of Portland, Ionia County

10 Upton Road, over the Maple River, 0.5 mile northwest of Elsie, Clinton County

11 Jones Road, over Stony Creek, 1.5 miles south of M-21, 4 miles southwest of Fowler, Clinton County

12 Fort Street, over the Power Canal, in Sault Ste. Marie, Chippewa County

13 County Road 510, over the Dead River, Negaunee Township, 3 miles north of US-41, Marquette County

14 Maple Road, over the Huron River, 1 mile north of M-14 northwest of Ann Arbor, Washtenaw County

15 Tallman Road, over the Looking Glass River, 3 miles west of Wacousta, Clinton County

16 Ingalls Road, over the Flat River, just south of Symrna, Ionia County

17 East Burt Road (Morseville Bridge), over the Flint River, just west of Morseville, Saginaw County

18 Sixth Street, over the Grand River, downtown Grand Rapids, Kent County

19 Maple Rapids Road, over the Maple River, 2 miles northwest of Elsie, Clinton County

20 Bridge Street, over the Grand River, city of Portland, Ionia County

21 Bell Road, over the Huron River, 1 mile north of Hudson Mills, Dexter Township, Washtenaw County

22 Sterling Road, over the St. Joseph River, 3 miles northwest of Jonesville, Hillsdale County

23 Six Mile Creek Road, over the Shiawassee River, 5 miles north of Owosso, 0.5 mile east of M-52, Shiawassee County

24 Buckner Road, over the St. Joseph River, just south of Mendon, St. Joseph County

25 Alaska Avenue, over the Thornapple River, 3 miles northeast of Caledonia, Kent County

26 $22\frac{1}{2}$ Mile Road, over the St. Joseph River, 2 miles west of Homer, Calhoun County

27 Smith's Crossing Road, over the Tittabawassee River, near Mapleton, Midland County

28 Shaytown Road, over Thornapple River, 2 miles east of Vermontville, Eaton County

29 Elm Circle Drive, over the Lower Rouge River, between John Daly and Inkster roads, north of Michigan Avenue, city of Inkster, Wayne County

30 Meskill Road, over the Belle River, 3 miles southeast of Memphis, St. Clair County

31 Hemlock Road, over the North Branch of the Bad River, 4 miles west of St. Charles, Saginaw County

32 M-65, over the Au Sable River, at Five Channels Dam, Iosco County

33 Twenty-One Mile Road, over Rice Creek, 3 miles northeast of Marshall, 1 mile north of I-94, Calhoun County

34 Welch Road, over Prairie Creek, 3 miles northeast of Ionia, Ionia County

35 Sorby Highway, over Fitts Creek, 1.5 miles south of Addison, between Manitou and Raymond streets, Lenawee County

36 Big Hill Road, over the Fawn River, 3 miles southeast of Sturgis, St. Joseph County

37 Balk Road, over the Fawn River, 4 miles southwest of Sturgis, St. Joseph County

38 Kelly Road, over the Muskegon River, Butterfield Township, 3 miles south of M-55, Missaukee County

39 Gorbell Road, over Hog Creek, 6 miles northeast of Coldwater, just east of US-27, Branch County

40 Holy Island Road, to Holy Island, over the South Arm of Lake Charlevoix, east of M-66, Charlevoix County

41 Armour Saari Road, over the Laughing Whitefish River, in Deerton, 2 miles south of M-28, Alger County

42 Glassman Road, over the Galien River, 3 miles northeast of New Buffalo, just east of I-94, Berrien County

43 Anton Street, over the Sebewaing River, just east of Back Street (M-25), Sebawaing, Huron County

44 Custer Road, over the Black River, 5 miles south of Deckerville, Sanilac County

45 West Main Street (Eagle River Road), over the Eagle River, Eagle River, Keweenaw County

46 West Verne Road, over Misteguay Creek, 3 miles west of Verne, Saginaw County

47 Rutledge Road, over the Munuscong River, northeast corner of Mackinac County

48 County Road 497, over the Sturgeon River, 6 miles north of Nahma Junction, Delta County

49 Downington Road, over the South Branch of the Cass River Drain, 14 miles west of Deckerville, Sanilac County

50 US-23, over the Ocqueoc River, 14 miles northwest of Rogers City, Presque Isle County

51 M-26 (Lakeshore Drive) over the Eagle River, Eagle River, Keweenaw County

52 Marquette Street, over the Penn Central Railroad, 0.75mile north of M-25, Bay City, Bay County

53 72nd Avenue, over White Creek, west of 52nd Street, 3 miles south of I-94, Van Buren County

54 Smith Road, over the Red Cedar River, 0.5 mile southeast of Fowlerville, just south of I-96, Livingston County

55 Teachout Road, over Wolf Creek, 2 miles southeast of Onsted, Lenawee County

56 Knight Highway, over the Black Creek, 3 miles northwest of Adrian, Lenawee County

57 Britain Avenue, over Second Valley Drive and Ox Creek, City of Benton Harbor, Berrien County

58 East Erie Street, over the South Branch of the Kalamazoo River, 3 miles east of Homer, Calhoun County

59 MacArthur Road, over Lake Creek, just south of Saranac, west of Morrison Lake Road, Ionia County

60 Beal City Road, South Branch of the Salt River, 4 miles northeast of Mount Pleasant, 3 miles east of US-27, Isabella County

61 57th Street, over the Kalamazoo River, New Richmond, 2 miles north of Fennville, Allegan County

62 Grosse Ile Bridge Road (Grosse Ile Toll Bridge) over the Trenton Channel, north end of channel, Wayne County

63 Grosse Ile Parkway, over the Trenton Channel, middle part of the channel, Wayne County

64 Fort Street, over the Rouge River, 0.25 mile northwest of the Rouge River (I-75) Bridge, Detroit, Wayne County

65 Dix Avenue, over the Rouge River, at the southern edge of the Ford Motor Company Rouge Complex, Dearborn, Wayne County

66 West Jefferson Avenue, over the Rouge River, in southwestern Detroit, at the Detroit-River Rouge border, Wayne County

67 Second Avenue, over the Thunder Bay River, city of Alpena, Alpena County

68 US-31, over the Manistee River, in the city of Manistee, Manistee County

69 US-41, over Portage Lake, between Houghton and Hancock, Houghton County

70 M-28, over the Middle Branch of the Ontonagon River, 4 miles west of Trout Creek, Ontonagon County

71 Ashmun Street, over the Power Canal, Sault Ste. Marie, Chippewa County

72 Interstate 75, over the St. Mary's River, Sault Ste. Marie, Chippewa County

73 M-55 (Mortimer E. Cooley) Bridge, over the Pine River, 21 miles east of Manistee, Manistee County

74 US-2, over the Cut River, 4 miles west of Brevort, Mackinac County

75 Interstate 69, 94 (Blue Water Bridge), over the St. Clair River, St. Clair County

76 Ambassador Bridge, over the Detroit River, Wayne County

77 Interstate 75, across the Straits of Mackinac, Mackinac and Emmet counties

78 Front Street, over the Boardman River, Traverse City, Grand Traverse County

79 West Michigan Avenue, over the Battle Creek River, in downtown Battle Creek, Calhoun County

80 McCamly Street, over the Battle Creek River, in downtown Battle Creek, Calhoun County

81 Twelve Mile Road, over the St. Joseph River, east of Burlington and south of M-60, Calhoun County

82 Michigan Railway Engineering Company (Interurban Walk) Bridge, over the Grand River, downtown Grand Rapids, Kent County

83 M-3, Southbound over the Clinton River, in Mt. Clemens, Macomb County

84 Elizabeth Park Drive, over the Elizabeth Park Canal, city of Trenton, Wayne County

85 Belle Isle (General MacArthur) Bridge, Foot of East Grand Boulevard in Detroit, over the Detroit River, to Belle Isle, Wayne County

86 M-69, over the Paint River, just east of Crystal Falls, Iron County

87 M-45 (Fulton Street), over the Grand River, downtown Grand Rapids, Kent County

88 Pine Island Drive, over the Rogue River, just north of 10 Mile Road, Kent County

89 Merrick Street, over the Raisin River, city of Adrian, 0.63 mile west of Main Street (M-52) and north of Beecher Road (M-34), Lenawee County

90 Ottawa Street, over the Muskegon River, just west of south approach to M-120 Causeway, at east end of Muskegon Lake, Muskegon County

91 County Road I-39, over the Rapid River, 7 miles north of Rapid River, Delta County

92 190th Avenue, over the Little Muskegon River, 1 mile southwest of Morley, Mecosta County

93 US-2, over the Manistique River, in Manistique, Schoolcraft County

94 Banat to Amberg Road (Chalk Hill Bridge), over the Menominee River, 5 miles west of Banat, Menominee County

95 West Mitchell Street, over Bear Creek, city of Petoskey, Emmet County

96 Old M-28, over the Rock River, 3 miles east of Covington, Baraga County

97 Portsmouth Road, over the Cheboyganing Drain, 2 miles north of M-81, northeast of Saginaw, Saginaw County

98 County Road 569, over the Sturgeon River, 3 miles east of Foster City, Dickinson County

99 Grange Road, over Stony Creek, 2 miles south of M-21, 3 miles southwest of Fowler, Clinton County

100 Okemos Road, over the Red Cedar River, downtown Okemos, Ingham County

101 US-12, over the St. Joseph River, in Mottville, St. Joseph County

102 M-32, over the Thunder Bay River, 9 miles east of Atlanta, Montmorency County

103 East Michigan Avenue, over the Kalamazoo River, east of Galesburg, Kalamazoo County

104 Genesee Road, over the Grand Trunk Western Railroad, in Lapeer, Lapeer County

105 Interstate 75, over the Rouge River, Detroit, Wayne County

106 Interstate 75 (Zilwaukee Bridge) over the Saginaw River, Zilwaukee, Saginaw County

LAKE SUPERIOR

KEWEENAW

HOUGHTON

ONTONAGON

BARAGA

MARQUETTE

GOGEBIC

IRON

DICKINSON

MENOMINEE

LAKE
MICHIGAN

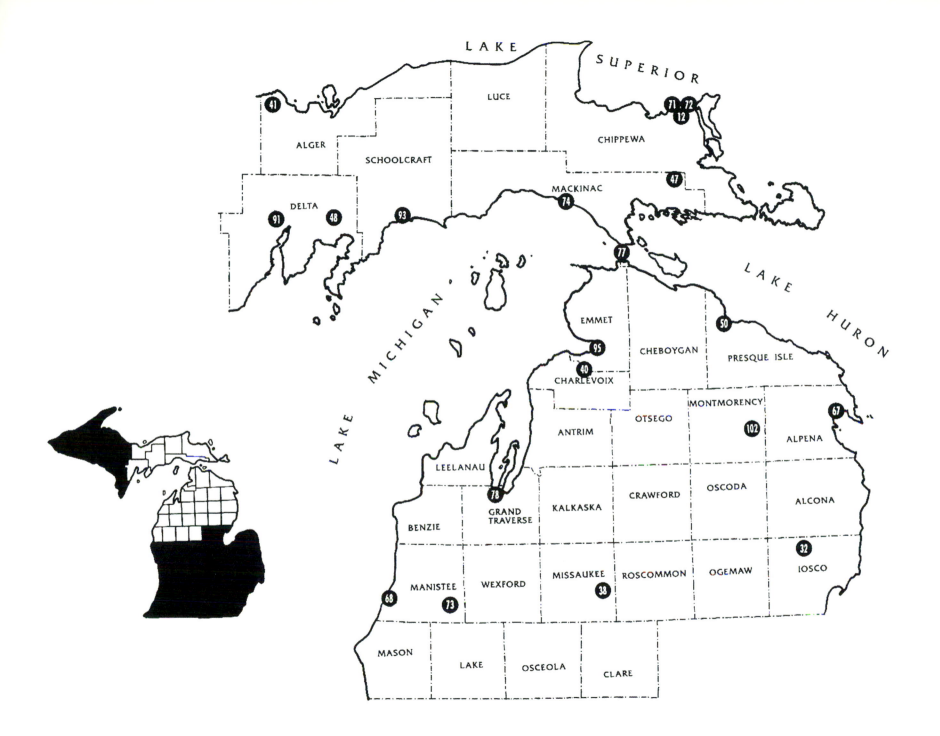

LAKE SUPERIOR

LAKE MICHIGAN

LAKE HURON

ALGER
LUCE
CHIPPEWA
SCHOOLCRAFT
DELTA
MACKINAC
EMMET
CHEBOYGAN
PRESQUE ISLE
CHARLEVOIX
MONTMORENCY
OTSEGO
ALPENA
ANTRIM
LEELANAU
CRAWFORD
OSCODA
ALCONA
GRAND TRAVERSE
KALKASKA
BENZIE
MANISTEE
WEXFORD
MISSAUKEE
ROSCOMMON
OGEMAW
IOSCO
MASON
LAKE
OSCEOLA
CLARE

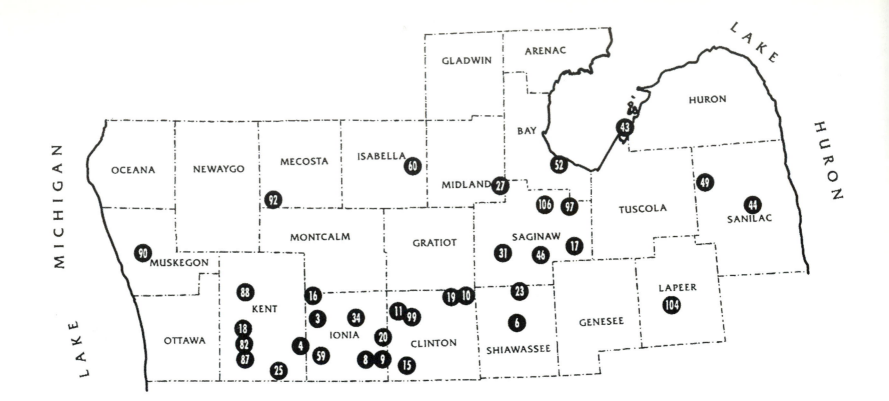

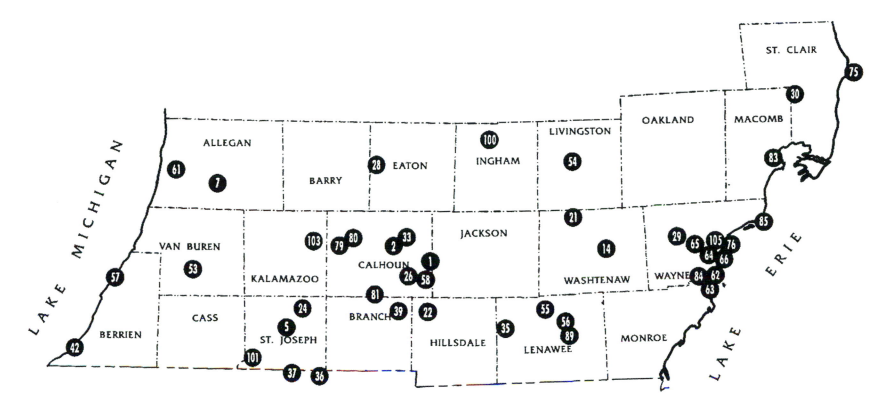

177

Appendix B

Builders of Michigan's Metal Truss Bridges

Bridge Company	Company Location	Number Built
American Bridge Co.	Chicago, Illinois	1
Attica Bridge Co.	Attica, Indiana	1
Brookville Bridge Co.	Brookville, Ohio	3
Buckeye Bridge Works	Cleveland, Ohio	1
Canton Bridge Co.	Canton, Ohio	2
Central State Bridge	Indianapolis, Indiana	1
Chicago Bridge & Iron	Chicago, Illinois	2
Continental Bridge Co.	Philadelphia, Pennsylvania	1
Detroit Bridge & Iron	Detroit, Michigan	2
Augustus J. Dupuis	Detroit, Michigan	1
Elkhart Bridge & Iron	Elkhart, Indiana	6
C. J. Glasgow	Detroit, Michigan	1
Groton Bridge & Mnfg.	Groton, New York	5
Illinois Bridge Co.	Chicago, Illinois	2
Jarvis Engineering	Lansing, Michigan	1

Bridge Company	Company Location	Number Built
Joliet Bridge & Iron	Joliet, Illinois	21
King Bridge Company	Cleveland, Ohio	38
Massillon Bridge Co.	Massillon, Ohio	19
Michigan Bridge Co.	Portland, Michigan	5
Michigan Bridge & Pipe	Lansing, Michigan	2
Minneapolis Bridge Co.	Minneapolis, Minnesota	1
Morse Bridge Company	Youngstown, Ohio	1
Mt. Vernon Bridge Co.	Mt. Vernon, Ohio	4
New Castle Bridge Co.	New Castle, Indiana	4
New Columbus Bridge Co.	Columbus, Ohio	1
New Jersey Bridge Co.	Manasquan, New Jersey	1
Northwestern Bridge & Iron	Milwaukee, Wisconsin	1
Ohio Bridge Company	Cleveland, Ohio	1
Penn Bridge Works	Beaver Falls, Pennsylvania	5
S. S. Ramsey	Portland, Michigan	2
Riverside Bridge Co.	Martin's Ferry, Ohio	1
Saginaw Bridge Co.	Saginaw, Michigan	1
Smith Bridge Co.,Toledo Bridge Company	Toledo, Ohio	8
Tunnel City Bridge & Iron	Port Huron, Michigan	1
Variety Ironworks	Cleveland, Ohio	3

Bridge Company	Company Location	Number Built
Wabash Bridge Co.	Wabash, Indiana	1
Wheaton Bridge Co.	Chicago, Illinois	3
Whitehead & Kales	River Rouge, Michigan	1
Wisconsin Bridge & Iron	Milwaukee, Wisconsin	3
Wrought Iron Bridge Co.	Canton, Ohio	50
Wynkoop & McGormley	(agents for Massillon Bridge Company)	2

Total Number Identified by Builder   **210**

Sources: The bulk of the information came from the surviving nameplates on the bridges. Useful general sources of information on a large number of bridge companies include the following: Victor C. Darnell, *Directory of American Bridge-Building Companies, 1840–1900* (Washington, D.C., 1984), *passim,* and Ohio Department of Transportation, *The Ohio Historic Bridge Inventory, Evaluation, and Preservation Plan* (Columbus, Ohio, 1983), pp. 220–225. Trade catalogues from two of the most important Ohio bridge companies were good sources of information on scores of bridges that no longer exist: King Iron Bridge and Manufacturing Company, *Catalogue* (Cleveland, 1884), and a similar publication from the same firm from around 1890; the Wrought Iron Bridge Company, *Book of Designs of Wrought Iron Bridges By the Wrought Iron Bridge Company of Canton, Ohio* (Canton, Ohio, 1874), *Illustrated Pamphlet of Wrought Iron Bridges Built by the Wrought Iron Bridge Company* (Canton, Ohio, 1885), and *Catalogue* (Canton, Ohio, ca. 1895). It is unfortunate that fewer than 40 of the 210 truss bridges identified by builder survive today.

Bibliography

Allen, Richard S. *Covered Bridges of the Middle West*. Brattleboro, Vt., 1970.

Anon. "Standard Bridge Plans of Michigan." *Municipal Journal* 42 (5 April 1917): 476–477.

———."Standard Reinforced Concrete Abutment of Michigan Highway Department." *Engineering and Contracting*, 25 April 1917, p. 401.

———."Winter Construction of Road Bridges in Michigan." *Engineering News-Record* 99 (8 December 1927): 914–916.

Ataman, Kathy. "Mottville's Camelback Bridge." *Michigan History* 65 (May/June 1981): 42–43.

Barrington, Edward. "Distinctive Features and Advantages of American Bridge Practice." *Michigan Engineer* 14 (1896): 155–173.

Bigelow, Lawrence N. "Fifty-Year Development—Construction of Steel Truss Bridges." American Society of Civil Engineers, *Journal of the Construction Division* 101 (June 1975): 239–258.

Billington, David P. "History and Esthetics in Concrete Arch Bridges." American Society of Civil Engineers, *Journal of the Structural Division* 103 (November 1977): 2129–2143.

Black, Archibald. *The Story of Bridges*. New York, 1936.

Boller, Alfred Pancoast. *Practical Treatise on the Construction of Iron Highway Bridges, for the Use of Town Committees*. New York, 1876.

Champion Bridge Company. *Catalogue*. Wilmington, Ohio, 1901.

Condit, Carl W. *American Building Art: The Nineteenth Century*. New York, 1960.

———. *American Building Art: The Twentieth Century*. New York, 1961.

Cooper, James L. *Iron Monuments to Distant Posterity: Indiana's Metal Bridges, 1870–1930*. Greencastle, Ind., 1987.

Danko, George M. "Development of the Truss Bridge, 1820-1930, With A Focus Toward Wisconsin." Ms., Madison, Wis., 1976.

Darnell, Victor C. *Directory of American Bridge-Building Companies, 1840–1900.* Washington, D.C., 1984.

Detroit Bridge and Iron Works. *Iron Bridges, Roofs, etc., as Built By the Detroit Bridge & Iron Works, of Detroit, Michigan.* Detroit, 1869.

Dewart, C. V. "Erecting Highway Bridges Under Traffic: Michigan." *Engineering News* 76 (26 November 1916): 798–799.

———. "Standard Bridge Plans of Michigan." *Municipal Journal* 42 (5 April 1917): 476–477.

———. "Standard Reinforced Concrete Abutment of Michigan Highway Department." *Engineering and Contracting* 47 (25 April 1917): 401.

———. "Standard Concrete Abutments For Michigan Bridges." *Engineering News* 76 (20 April 1916): 738–739.

———. "Standard Pony-Truss Bridges For Michigan Highways." *Engineering News* 76 (23 November 1916): 990.

Dunbar, Willis F. *All Aboard! A History of Railroads in Michigan.* Grand Rapids, 1969.

Dunbar, Willis F., and George S. May. *Michigan: A History of the Wolverine State.* Rev. ed. Grand Rapids, 1980.

Duncan, W. J. "Bridge Building, Past and Present." *Michigan Engineer* 14 (1896): 174–196.

Earle, Horatio Sawyer. *The Autobiography of "By Gum" Earle.* Lansing, 1929.

Edwards, Llewellyn Nathaniel. *A Record of the History and Evolution of Early American Bridges.* Orono, Maine, 1959.

Gies, Joseph. *Bridges and Men.* Garden City, N.J., 1963.

Gray, George E. "Notes on the Early Practice in Bridge Building." American Society of Civil Engineers, *Transactions* 37 (June 1897): 1–16.

Greene, C. E. "Highway Bridges From the Point of View of the Public." *Michigan Engineer* 6 (1888): 74–83.

Haupt, Herman. *General Theory of Bridge Construction.* New York, 1851.

Hool, George Albert, ed. *Moveable and Long-Span Bridges.* New York, 1923.

Hool, George Albert, and W. A. Kine, eds. *Reinforced Concrete and Masonry Structures.* New York, 1924.

Hopkins, Henry J. *A Span of Bridges: An Illustrated History.* New York, 1970.

Hovey, Otis Ellis. *Moveable Bridges.* Volume I: *Superstructure.* Volume II: *Machinery.* New York, 1926.

Illinois Bridge Company. *Bridges of Concrete and What They Cost.* Chicago, 1914.

Illinois Highway Commission. *Modern Bridges For Illinois Highways.* 2nd ed. Springfield, Ill., 1912.

Imberman, Eli Woodruff. "The Formative Years of the Chicago Bridge and Iron Company." Ph.D. diss., University of Chicago, 1973.

Indiana Bridge Company. *Indiana Bridge: A Hoosier Tradition.* Muncie, Ind., 1952.

Jackson, Donald C. *Great American Bridges and Dams.* Washington, D.C., 1988.

———. "Railroads, Truss Bridges and the Rise of the Civil Engineer." *Civil Engineering* 47 (October 1977): 97–101.

———. "The Thacher Truss." Society For Industrial Archeology *Newsletter* 9 (January/March 1979): 9.

Ketchum, Milo Smith. *The Design of Highway Bridges and the Calculation of Stress in Bridge Trusses.* New York, 1909.

King Iron Bridge and Manufacturing Company. *Catalogue.* Cleveland, 1884.

———. *Catalogue.* Cleveland, ca. 1890.

Kirkham, John Edward. *Highway Bridges: Design and Cost.* New York, 1932.

Mason, Philip Parker. *The Ambassador Bridge: A Monument to Progress.* Detroit, 1987.

———. "Horatio S. Earle and the Good Roads Movement in Michigan." *Papers of the Michigan Academy of Science, Arts and Letters* 43 (1958): 269–279.

———. "The League of American Wheelmen and the Good-Roads Movement, 1880–1905." Ph.D. diss., University of Michigan, 1958.

McCullough, Conde B. *Economics of Highway Bridge Types.* Chicago, 1929.

Melick, C. A. "Old Steel Road Bridges Restored By Welding." *Engineering News-Record* 106 (1 June 1933): 706–708.

———. "Record of the Work of Bridge Building By State." *Michigan Roads and Pavements* 19 (22 November 1922): 12–14.

———. "Standard Bridge Practice of the Michigan State Highway Department." *Concrete* 23 (July 1923): 3–10 and 23 (August 1923): 69–74.

———. "Summary of the Work of the Bridge Department." *Michigan Roads and Pavements* 23 (1 January 1925): 29–30.

Miars, David H. *A Century of Bridges: The History of the Champion Bridge Company and the Development of Industrial Manufacturing in Wilmington, Ohio.* Wilmington, Ohio, 1972.

Michigan Department of Transportation. *Making Michigan Move: A History of Michigan Highways and the Michigan Department of Transportation.* Lansing, 1980.

———. *The Zilwaukee Bridge: From the Beginning.* Lansing, 1987.

Michigan Roads and Pavements. "20 Years of Roadbuilding Programs in Michigan and the United States, 1905–1925." Lansing, 1925.

Michigan State Highway Committee. *Report of the State Highway Committee Established by the Legislature of 1901 and Appointed by His Excellency, Aaron T. Bliss, Governor.* Lansing, 1903.

Michigan State Highway Commission. *Biennial Report.* Lansing, 1907–.

———. *Standard Road and Bridge Specifications.* Lansing, 1926.

Morrison, Roger L. *The History and Development of Michigan Highways.* Ann Arbor, 1938.

Older, Clifford. "Kentucky Road Department Has Standard Bridges." *Engineering News-Record* 79 (9 August 1917): 255.

———. "Standard Plans Solve Problems of State Highway Bridge Supervision in Illinois." *Engineering News-Record* 78 (5 April 1917): 31–34.

Peters, Kenneth Earl. "The Good-Road Movement and the Michigan State Highway Department, 1905–1917." Ph.D. diss., University of Michigan, 1972.

Plowden, David. *Bridges: The Spans of North America.* New York, 1974.

Rae, John B. *The American Automobile: A Brief History.* Chicago, 1965.

Ratigan, William. *Highways Over Broad Waters: The Life and Times of David B. Steinman, Bridgebuilder.* Grand Rapids, 1959.

Rogers, Frank Foster. *The History of the Michigan State Highway Department, 1905–1933.* Lansing, 1933.

Rubin, Lawrence A. *Bridging the Straits: The Story of the Mighty Mac.* Detroit, 1985.

———. *Mighty Mac: The Official Picture History of the Mackinac Bridge.* Detroit, 1986.

Sears, William B. "Highways and Highway Bridges." *Michigan Engineer* 6 (1888): 48–57.

Seely, Bruce F. *Building the American Highway System: Engineers as Policy Makers.* Philadelphia, 1987.

———. "Engineers and Government-Business Cooperation: Highway Standards and the Bureau of Public Roads, 1900-1940." *Business History Review* 58 (Spring 1984): 51–77.

———. "Highway Engineers as Policy Makers: The Bureau of Public Roads." Ph.D. diss., University of Delaware, 1982.

Steinman, David B. *Fifty Years of Progress in Bridge Engineering.* New York, 1929.

———. *Miracle Bridge at Mackinac.* Grand Rapids, 1957.

Steinman, David B., and Sara Ruth Watson. *Bridges and Their Builders.* New York, 1941.

Stimson, G. K. "Historic Background of Michigan Transportation." *Michigan Roads and Pavements* 22 (29 October 1925): 36–48.

Taylor, Frederick Winslow, Sanford E. Thompson, and Edward Smulski. *Reinforced Concrete Bridges.* London, 1939.

Taylor, George Rogers. *The Transportation Revolution.* New York, 1951.

Thacher, Edwin. "Concrete and Concrete-Steel in the United States." A.S.C.E. *Transactions* 54, Part E (1905): 426–458.

Thurber, Pamela. "The Groton Iron Bridge Company." *Historic Ithaca,* Fall 1983, pp. I–IV.

Tyrrell, Henry Grattan. *History of Bridge Engineering.* Chicago, 1911.

United States Department of War, U.S. Army, Corps of Engineers. *List of Bridges Over the Navigable Waters of the United States, 1925.* Washington, D.C., 1926.

Veddar, H. K. "Highway Bridges in the Manufacturer's Hands." *Michigan Engineer* 13 (1895): 135–142.

Waddell, John Alexander Low. *Bridge Engineering.* 2 vols. New York, 1916.

———. *The Designing of Ordinary Highway Bridges.* New York, 1884.

———. *Economics of Bridgework, A Sequel To Bridge Engineering.* New York, 1921.

———. *De Pontibus: A Pocket-Book For Bridge Engineers.* 2nd ed. New York, 1898.

———. *The Principal Professional Papers of Dr. J.A.L. Waddell, Civil Engineer.* Edited by John Lyle Harrington. New York, 1905.

Weale, John, ed. *The Theory, Practice, and Architecture of Bridges of Stone, Iron, Timber, and Wire.* 2 vols. London, 1843.

Whitney, Charles S. *Bridges: Their Art, Science, and Evolution.* New York, 1983.

Wrought Iron Bridge Company. *Book of Designs of Wrought Iron Bridges By The Wrought Iron Bridge Company of Canton, Ohio.* Canton, Ohio, 1876.

———. *Illustrated Pamphlet of Wrought Iron Bridges Built By The Wrought Iron Bridge Company.* Canton, Ohio, 1885.

———. *Wrought Iron Bridges Built By The Wrought Iron Bridge Company.* Fitchburg, Mass., 1885.

———. *Catalogue.* Canton, Ohio, ca. 1895.

Index

References to photographs and drawings are printed in boldface type.

Addison, 82
Adrian, 91, 127
Advisory Council on Historic Preservation, 10
Air-entrainment of concrete, 145
Alaska Avenue bridge (Kent County), 76
Albion, 51
Alger County, 84
Allegan, 12, 14, 67
Allegan County, 12, 67, 93
Alpena, 101
Alpena County, 101
Ambassador Bridge (Detroit), 109, **109**, 147–50, **149**
American Bridge Company (Chicago, Ill.), 31, 93, 101, 152, 179
American Bridge Division, U. S. Steel Corporation, 111, 165
American Institute of Steel Construction Award, 101, 106
American Transit Company, 148
Ammann, Othmar H., 161
Ann Arbor, 32, 73
Anton Street bridge (Huron County), 84
Armour Saari Road bridge (Alger County), 84
Ashmun Street Bridge (Sault Ste. Marie), 104, **104–5**
Attica Bridge Company (Attica, Ind.), 76, 179
Au Sable River, 81
Au Sable River bridge (Mio), **41**
Austin, James W., 148

Bad River, 80
Baldwin, E. W. (St. Louis, Mich.), 132
Balk Road bridge (St. Joseph County), 83
Baltimore truss, 62, 70, **70**
Banat to Amberg Road (Chalk Hill) bridge (Menominee County), 132, **132–33**

Baraga County, 135
Battle Creek, 117
Battle Creek River, 117
Bay City, 32, 90
Bay County, 90
Beach Manufacturing Company (Charlotte, Mich.), 90
Beal City Road bridge (Isabella County), 92
Bear River, 133
Belle Isle (General MacArthur) Bridge (Detroit), 123, **123–24**
Belle River, 80
Belleville bridge (Wayne County), 13
Bell Road bridge (Washtenaw County), 75
Benton Harbor, 91
Berrien County, 84, 91
Bethlehem Steel Company, 152
Big Hill Road bridge (St. Joseph County), 83, **83**
Black Creek, 91
Black River, 84
Bliss, Aaron, 33, 34
Blue Water Bridge (Port Huron), **108**, 109, **150–51**, 152
Boardman River, 117
Bodner, Pierce, 59
Bois Blanc Island, 160
Boller, Alfred P., 24; *Practical Treatise on the Construction of Iron Highway Bridges for the Use of Town Committees,* 24
Bollman Truss, 64
Bower, James A., 148
Branch County, 84
Brazee, Jared N., 24, 57, 58
Brevort, 106
Bridge Street bridge (Portland), 12, **25**, 75, **75–76**
Britain Avenue bridge (Benton Harbor), 91
Brooklyn Bridge, 62, 89
Brookville Bridge Company (Brookville, Ohio), 179

Brown, Josiah, 57
Brown, Prentis M., 160–61, 165
Brown Truss, 57
Buckeye Bridge Works (Cleveland, Ohio), 179
Buckner Road bridge (St. Joseph County), 76
Bureau of History, Michigan Department of State, 7, 9, 10, 14
Burlington, 118
Burr Truss, 53

C & O Railroad, 91
Caledonia, 76
Calhoun County, 51, 77, 82, 92, 117, 118
Canadian Transit Company, 148
Canton Bridge Company (Canton, Ohio), 179
Cass River Drain, 85
Central State Bridge Company (Indianapolis, Ind.), 84, 179
Chalk Hill bridge (Menominee County). *See* Banat to Amberg Road bridge
Champion Bridge Company (Wilmington, Ohio), 30
Charlevoix County, 84
Cheboygan, 160
Cheboyganing Drain, 135
Chicago Bascule Bridge Company, 100
Chicago Bridge & Iron Company (Chicago, Ill.), 179
"Chicago Type" trunnion style bascule bridge, 99
Chippewa County, 70, 104
Cissell, James E., 160
Clinton County, 68, 70, 73, 136
Clinton River, 121
Coldwater, 84
Commonwealth Associates, 118
Comstock, Governor William A., 160
Connections, pinned, **63**, 64
Connections, riveted, **63**, 64

Continental Bridge Company (Philadelphia, Pa.), 179
Cooley, Mortimer E., 106
Cooley (Mortimer E.) Bridge (Manistee County), 12, 43, **43**, 106, **107**
County Road 497 bridge (Delta County), 85
County Road 510 bridge (Marquette County), 70, **72**
County Road 569 bridge (Dickenson County), 135
County Road I-39 bridge (Delta County), 131
County road commissions, 21, 34
Covington, 135
Critical Bridge Fund, 8
Crystal Falls, 123
Custer Road bridge (Sanilac County), 84
Cut River, 106
Cut River (US-2) Bridge (Mackinac County), 12, 106, **108**

Darnell, Victor, 27, 29
Davison, L. A. & Company, 135
Dead River, 70
Deckerville, 84, 85
Deerton, 84
Dehmel Road bridge (Saginaw County), 13
Delta Contracting Company (Escanaba), 131
Delta County, 85, 131
Denny, Grover C., 165
Department of Transportation Act, 8
Detroit and Milwaukee Railroad, 19
Detroit Bridge & Iron Works (Detroit, Mich.), 29, 68, 179
Detroit Industrial Expressway, 143
Detroit International Bridge Company, 148–49, 152
Detroit, Mackinac and Marquette Railroad, 159
Detroit River, 19, 109, 123, 147–50
Detroit River railroad tunnel, 147
Detroit-Windsor Vehicular Tunnel, 147, 152
Dewart, C. V., 35, 36, 38, 39, 41
"Dewart's tunnels," 36
Dickinson County, 135
Dillman, Grover, 35
Ditch Road bridge (Saginaw County), **63**, 64
Dix Avenue bascule bridge (Wayne County), 12, 100
Double-intersection Pratt (Whipple) truss, 62, 64, **65–67**
Downington Road bridge (Sanilac County), 85
Dupuis, Augustus J. (Detroit, Mich.), 94, 179

Eads Bridge (St. Louis, Missouri), 62, 89
Eads, James B., 47, 62
Eagle River, 11, 84, 86
Eagle River Historic District, 11
Eagle River Road (Eagle River) bridge. *See* West Main Street bridge
Earle, Horatio S., **33**, 33–35
East Burt Road (Morseville) bridge (Saginaw County), 73
East Cass Street bridge (Albion), 51, **51**
East Erie Street bridge (Calhoun County), 92
East Michigan Avenue bridge (Kalamazoo County), 137
East Sheridan Road bridge (Saginaw County), 13
Eaton County, 77

Electric interurban railroads, 32
Elizabeth Park Canal, 121
Elizabeth Park Drive bridge (Trenton), 121, **121**
Elkhart Bridge & Iron Company (Elkhart, Ind.), 77, 84, 179
Elm Circle Drive Bridge (Wayne County), 80, **80–81**
Elsie, 73
Ely, Townsend A., 35
Emmet County, 111, 133

Fallasburg Bridge (Kent County), **22**, 58, **58**
Fargo Engineering Company, Kalamazoo, 118
Fawn River, 83
Federal Aid Road Act of 1916, 35, 38
Federal Highway Administration, 9, 13, 166
Fennville, 93
57th Street bridge (Allegan County), **63**, 93, **96**
Fink Truss, 64
Fitts Creek, 82
Five Channels Dam, 81
Flat River, 57, 58, 73
Flint River, 73
Ford (Edsel B.) Expressway, 143
Ford Motor Company River Rouge complex, 93, 100
Fort Street (Old US-25) bridge (Wayne County), 100
Fort Street bridge (Sault Ste. Marie), 70
Foster City, 135
Fowler, 136
Fowler, Charles Evan, 148, 160
Fowlerville, 90
Frankenmuth, 13
Front Street bridge (Grand Traverse County), 117
Fry & Kain, Inc., 104
Fulton Street (M-45) bridge (Grand Rapids), 123, 125, **125–26**

Galesburg, 137
Galien River, 84
General MacArthur Bridge. *See* Belle Isle Bridge
Genesee Road bridge (Lapeer County), 137
George Washington Bridge, 150
Glasgow, C. J. (Detroit, Mich.), 80, 179
Glassman Road bridge (Berrien County), 84
"Good-roads" movement, 33
Goodwin Bridge (Portland), **25**
Gorbell Road bridge (Branch County), 84
"Governor's Walk" (Mackinac Bridge Walk), 165
Graham, David (Minnesota), 135
Grand Haven, 19
Grand Hotel, Mackinac Island, 160
Grand Rapids, 14, 32, 73, 118, 123
Grand Rapids & Indiana Railway, 159
Grand River, 19, 47, 48, 68, 70, 73, 75, 118, 123
Grand River Avenue bridge (Novi), **139–40**
Grand River bridge (Grand Ledge), **115–16**
Grand River bridge (Saranac), **28**
Grand Traverse County, 117
Grand Trunk Western Railroad, 137, 147
Grange Road bridge (Clinton County), 136

Great Depression, 32, 152
Great Western Railway, 147
Green, Governor Fred, 149
Grosse Ile Bridge Road bridge (Wayne County). *See* Grosse Ile Toll Bridge
Grosse Ile Parkway bridge (Wayne County), 94, **98**
Grosse Ile Toll (Grosse Ile Bridge Road) Bridge (Wayne County), 94, **97**
Groton Bridge & Manufacturing Company (Groton, N.Y.), 30, 75, 179
Groves & Sons, S. J. (Minneapolis), 168

Hall Electric Company, 101
Haltenhoff, C. E., 111
Hancock, 152
HD Road bridge (Marquette County), **63**, **85**
Hemlock Road bridge (Saginaw County), 80
Hicks Construction Company (Iron Mountain), 114
Hillsdale County, 75
Historic American Engineering Record Collection, 13
Hog Creek, 84
Holy Island Road bridge (Charlevoix County), 84
Homer, 77, 92
Houghton, 152
Houghton County, 101
Houghton-Hancock bridge (Houghton County), 101, 152, **153–56**, 159
Howe Truss, 53, **54**, 58, 59
Howe, William, 53
Hudson, Robert, 104
Huron County, 84
Huron River, 19, 73, 75
Huron River bridge (Dexter), **26**
Huron River bridge (Vassar), **20**
Hyde, Charles K., 9

Illinois Bridge Company (Chicago, Ill.), 114, 118, 179
Illinois Highway Commission, 38
Indian River bridge (Indian River), **37**
Ingalls Road bridge (Ionia County), 73
Ingham County, 136
Inkster, 80
Intermodal Surface Transportation Efficiency Act of 1991, 11, 14
International (Interstate 75) Bridge (Sault Ste. Marie), 104, 106, **157–58**, 159
International Bridge Authority, 159
International Walkers Association, 165
Interstate 69, 94 bridge (Port Huron). *See* Blue Water Bridge
Interstate 75 bridge (Detroit). *See* Rouge River Bridge
Interstate 75 bridge (Emmet and Mackinac Counties). *See* Mackinac Straits Bridge
Interstate 75 bridge (Sault Ste. Marie). *See* International Bridge
Interstate Highway Act, 143
Interurban Walk (Michigan Railway Engineering Company) bridge (Grand Rapids), 118
Ionia, 82

Ionia County, 11, 13, 57, 68, 73, 75, 82, 92
Iosco County, 81
Iron County, 123
Isabella County, 92

Jackson, Donald C., 9
Jacobson, George, 152
Jarvis Engineering (Lansing, Mich.), 179
Johnson Construction Company, Al, 101, 152
Joliet Bridge & Iron Company (Joliet, Ill.), 31, 77, 84, 85, 180
Jones, Jonathan, 109, 148
Jones Road bridge (Clinton County), 70, **70–71**
Joy, James F., 148

Kalamazoo, 19, 32
Kalamazoo County, 137
Kalamazoo River, 19, 51, 67, 92, 93, 137
Kellogg Truss, 62
Kelly Road bridge (Missaukee County), 83
Kent County, 13, 24, 58, 73, 76, 118, 123, 127
Kent Street (Townline) bridge (Ionia County), 68
Keweenaw County, 84, 86
Keweenaw Peninsula, 11, 159
Keweenaw Waterway, 159
King Bridge Company (Cleveland, Ohio), 31, 67, 180
King post truss, 53, **53–54**
Kinney, J. W., 165
Knight Highway bridge (Lenawee County), 91
Kutche, A. W. and Company, 121

Lake Carriers Association, 148
Lake Charlevoix, 84
Lake Creek, 92
Lakeshore Drive (M-26) bridge (Eagle River), 86, **86**
Langley Bridge (St. Joseph County), 59
Lansing, 47, 48
Lapeer, 137
Lapeer County, 137
League of American Wheelmen, 33
Lemon, Jack, 127
Lenawee County, 82, 91, 127
Lenticular truss, 64
Leonard Street bridge (Grand Rapids), **56**
Little Muskegon River, 132
Livingston County, 90
Lodge (John C.) Expressway, 143
Looking Glass River, 73

M-3 bridge (Mt. Clemens), **119–20**, 120–21
M-26 bridge (Eagle River). *See* Lakeshore Drive bridge
M-28 bridge (Ontonagon County), 102, **102–3**
M-32 Spur bridge (Montmorency County), 137, **138**
M-45 bridge (Grand Rapids). *See* Fulton Street bridge
M-55 bridge (Manistee County). *See* Cooley, Mortimer E. Bridge
M-65 bridge (Iosco County), **42**, 81, **81**
M-69 bridge (Crystal Falls), 123

MacArthur Road bridge (Ionia County), 92
McCamly Street bridge (Calhoun County), 117
McClintic-Marshall Company, 109, 148–49
McGrath, Martin, 152
Mackinac Bridge Authority, 111, 161
Mackinac Bridge Citizens Committee, 160
Mackinac Bridge Walk ("Governor's Walk"), 165
Mackinac County, 12, 84, 106, 111
Mackinac Island, 159–60
Mackinac Straits (Interstate 75) Bridge (Emmet and Mackinac Counties), 111, **111**, 159–64, **161–64**
Mackinac Straits Bridge Authority, 160
Mackinac Transportation Company, 159
Mackinaw City, 160
McMath, Francis C., 160
Macomb County, 121
Mahan Company, R. C., 101
Manistee, 101
Manistee County, 12, 43, 101, 106
Manistee River, 12, 101
Manistique, 132
Manistique River, 132
Manistique River bridge (Gerfask), **36**
Maple Rapids Road bridge (Clinton County), 73
Maple River, 73
Maple River bridge (Ionia County), **113**
Maple Road bridge (Washtenaw County), 73
Mapleton, 77
Marquette County, 35, 70
Marquette Street bridge (Bay County), 90–91, **91**
Marshall, 51, 82
Marshall, William and Son (Grand Rapids), 137
Massillon Bridge Company (Massillon, Ohio), 31, 73, 76, 82, 180
Meads and Anderson, 102
Meager and Sons, W. J., 106
Mecosta County, 132
Melick, C. A., 39, 41
Memphis, 80
Mendon, 76
Menominee County, 132
Menominee River, 132
Merrick Street Bridge (Adrian), 127, **129–30**
Merritt-Chapman and Scott Corporation (New York), 111, 165
Meskill Road bridge (St. Clair County), 80
Michigamme, 35
Michigan Avenue (Lansing), 47
Michigan Avenue bridge (Lansing), **48–49**
Michigan Bridge Company (Portland, Mich.), 180
Michigan Bridge and Pipe Company (Lansing, Mich.), 180
Michigan Central Railroad, 19, 94, 147, 159
Michigan Department of Transportation, 8–14, 146, 166, 168
Michigan Department of Transportation, Local Services Division, 9
Michigan Railway Engineering Company bridge (Grand Rapids). *See* Interurban Walk bridge
Michigan Southern Railroad, 19

Michigan state attorney general, 34
Michigan state highway commissioner, 34, 143
Michigan State Highway Department, 33, 35, 38, 41, 43, 70, 86, 101–2, 104, 106, 114, 123, 131, 133, 135–37, 143, 145–46, 161
Michigan State Normal School, 32
Michigan State Senate, 34
Michigan state trunkline system, 34–35
Midland County, 77
Military Street bridge (Port Huron), **92–93**, 99
Minneapolis Bridge Company (Minneapolis, Minn.), 180
Missaukee County, 83
Mississippi River, 47
Missouri Valley Bridge and Iron Company, 100
Misteguay Creek, 84
Modjeski and Masters, 152, 160
Moisseiff, Leon S., 160
Monroe, 19
Monroe Construction Company (Charlevoix), 117
Monsarrat and Pratley, 152
Montmorency County, 137
Monzani, Willoughby, 62
Morley, 132
Morse Bridge Company (Youngstown, Ohio), 76, 180
Morseville, 73
Morseville bridge (Saginaw County). *See* East Burt Road bridge
Mottville, 11, 136
Mottville (US-12) Bridge (St. Joseph County), 136, **136–37**
Mount Hope Bridge (Narraganset Bay, Rhode Island), 149
Mt. Pleasant, 92
Mt. Vernon Bridge Company (Mt. Vernon, Ohio), 180
Munuscong River, 84
Muskegon, 32
Muskegon County, 131
Muskegon Lake, 131
Muskegon River, 83, 131
Muskegon River bridge (Big Rapids), **21**

Nahma Junction, 85
National Historic Preservation Act of 1966, 7, 8
National Register of Historic Places, 7, 8, 9, 10
New Buffalo, 84
New Castle Bridge Company (New Castle, Ind.), 70, 180
New Columbus Bridge Company (Columbus, Ohio), 180
New Jersey Bridge Company (Manasquan, N.J.), 180
Nolan, E. C. & Son (Detroit), 114
North Park Street bridge (Kent County), 13
Northwestern Bridge & Iron Company (Milwaukee, Wis.), 180

Oakwood Avenue bridge (Owosso), 64, **65–66**
Ocquenoc River, 85
Ohio Bridge Company (Cleveland, Ohio), 180
Okemos, 136
Okemos Road bridge (Ingham County), 136
Old M-28 bridge (Baraga County), 135
Old US-25 bridge (Wayne County). *See* Fort Street bridge

190th Avenue bridge (Mecosta County), 132
Onstead, 91
Ontonagon County, 101
Ontonagon River, 102
Ontonagon River Bridge (Watersmeet), **20**
Osborne, Chase, 160
Ottawa Street bridge (Muskegon County), 131, **131**
Owosso, 64, 76
Ox Creek, 91

Paint River, 123
Parker Truss, 62, 67, **68–69**, 80–81, **81**
Pearl Street bridge (Grand Rapids), **2**
Pechekee River, 35
Penn Bridge Works (Beaver Falls, Pa.), 30, 73, 82, 180
Penn Central Railroad, 90
Pennsylvania Truss, 62, 70, **72**
Petoskey, 133
Philadelphia and Reading Railroad, 59
Pine Island Drive bridge (Kent County), **34**, 127, **127–28**
Pine River, 106
Plainwell bridge (Allegan County), **114**
Pontiac, 19
Population, Detroit, 19, 31
Population, Michigan, 19, 31
Port Huron, 32, 109, 152
Portage Lake, 101, 152, 159
Portland, 13, 14, 68, 75
Portsmouth Road bridge (Saginaw County), 135
Prairie Creek, 82
Pratt Truss, 62, **73**, 73–77, 82–83
Presque Isle County, 85
Price Brothers (Lansing), 136
Public Works Administration, 160

Railroads, 19, 32, 47
Raisin River, 19, 127
Raisin River bridges (Blissfield), **59**
Ramsey, S. S. (Portland, Mich.), 180
Ransome, Ernest, 112
Rapid River, 131
Rapid River bridge (Antrim County), **39**
Red Cedar River, 90, 136
Reinhardt, Morris C., 9
Rice Creek, 82
Riverside Bridge Company (Martin's Ferry, Ohio), 180
River Street bridge (Lansing), 48
Rock River, 135
Roebling, John, 62, 89
Rogers City, 85
Rogers, Frank F., 35, **35**
Rogue [sic] River, 127
Romney, Governor George, 165
Roosevelt, President Franklin D., 160
Rouge River, 80, 93, 100, 145
Rouge River (Interstate 75) Bridge (Detroit), **144–45**, 145
Round Island, 160

Rush Street bridge (Chicago, Ill.), 93
Rutledge Road bridge (Mackinac County), 84

Saginaw, 135
Saginaw Bridge Company (Saginaw, Mich.), 180
Saginaw County, 13, 73, 80, 84, 135
Saginaw River, 19, 166, 168
St. Charles, 80
St. Clair County, 80, 109
St. Clair River, 19, 109
St. Clair River tunnel, 147
St. Ignace, 160
St. Joseph County, 59, 76, 83, 136
St. Joseph River, 59, 75, 76, 77, 118, 136
St. Joseph River bridge (Niles), **60–61**
St. Louis, Missouri, 47
St. Mary's River, 104, 159
Salt River, 92
Sanilac County, 84, 85
Saranac, 92
Sarnia Bridge Company, 152
Sarnia, Ontario, 109, 152
Sault Ste. Marie, Michigan, 104, 159
Sault Ste. Marie, Ontario, 159
Scherzer bascule bridge, 12
Scherzer Rolling Lift Bridge Company, 101
Schoolcraft County, 132
Sebawaing, 84
Sebawaing River, 84
Second Avenue bridge (Alpena), 101
Second Street bridge (Allegan), 12, 67, **67**
72nd Avenue Bridge (Van Buren County), 90
Shaytown Road bridge (Eaton County), 77
Sheffield Bridge (Three Rivers), **54**
Sherman Anti-Trust Act, 31
Shiawassee County, 64, 76
Shiawassee River, 64, 76
Shiawassee River bridge (Owosso), **29**
Sioems, Helmers, & Schaffer (St. Paul, Minnesota), 132
"Siphon" (US-2) Bridge (Manistique), 132
Six Mile Creek Road bridge (Shiawassee County), 76
Sixth Street bridge (Grand Rapids), 73, **74**
Smith & Nichols (Hastings, Mich.), 136
Smith Bridge Company, Toledo Bridge Company (Toledo, Ohio), 73, 75, 84, 180
Smith-Holmes-Burridge-Sparks, 123
Smith Road bridge (Livingston County), 90
Smith's Crossing bridge (Midland County), 77, **77–78**
Smith-Wynkoop & McGormley, 82
Smyrna, 57, 73
Sorby Highway Bridge (Lenawee County), 82
South Marshall Avenue bridge (Marshall), 51, **52**
State Historic Preservation Office, 9
State Historic Preservation Officers, 7
State Reward Act of 1919, 35
State Reward Law of 1905, 34
State Reward Roads, 35

State Trunk Line Act of 1913, 34, 35
Statute labor system, 20
Steinman, Boyton, Gronquist, and London, 159
Steinman, David B., 111, 149, 161, 165
Sterling Road bridge (Hillsdale County), 75
Stevin Construction (the Netherlands), 168
Stony Creek, 136
Storen Company, W. J., 101
Straits of Mackinac, 111, 159–160
Strom Construction Company, 101
Sturgeon River, 85, 135
Sturgis, 83
Surface Transportation and Uniform Relocation Assistance Act of 1987, 10, 13

Tacoma Narrows Bridge (Wash. State), 160
Tallman Road bridge (Clinton County), 73
Teachout Road bridge (Lenawee County), 91
Thacher, Edwin, 64
Thacher Truss, **63**, 64
Thornapple River, 76, 77
Thornapple River bridge (Kent County), **22**
Thunder Bay River, 101, 137
Tittabawassee River, 77
Tittabawassee River bridge (Midland), **30–31**
Tobacco River bridge (Gladwin County), **27**
Toebe Construction Company, Walter (Wixom, Mich.), 168
Town, Ithiel, 53
Town Lattice Truss, 53, **54**
Townline (Kent Street) bridge (Ionia County), 69
Traverse City, 117
Trenton, 121
Trenton Channel, 94
Truss bedstead, 79, 80
Truss types: Bollman, 64; bowstring arch, **60**, 62, 80–81; Burr, 53; cantilevered steel, 106–9, **106–8**; double-intersection Pratt, 62, 64, **65–67**; Howe, 53, **54**, 58–59; Kellogg, 62; king post, 53, **53–54**; lenticular, 64; Parker, 62, 67, **68–69**, 80–81, **81**; Pennsylvania, 62, 70, **72**; Pratt, 62, **73–77**, 73–78, 82–83, **82–83**; Thacher, **63**, 64; Town Lattice, 53, **54**; truss bedstead, 79, 80; Warren, 62, 77–78, **78**, 84–85; Whipple, 62, 64, **65–67**
Tunnel City Bridge & Iron Company (Port Huron, Mich.), 180
Turner Road bridge, 68
Twelve Mile Road bridge (Calhoun County), 82, **82**, 118, **118**
22 1/2 Mile Road bridge (Calhoun County), 77
US-2 bridge (Mackinac County). See Cut River Bridge
US-2 bridge (Manistique). See "Siphon" Bridge
US-12 bridge (St. Joseph County). See Mottville Bridge
US-23 bridge (Arenac County), **38**
US-23 bridge (Au Sable), **40**
US-23 bridge (Presque Isle County), 85
US-31 bridge (Grand Haven), **95**
US-31 bridge (Manistee), 12, **100**, 101
US-31 bridge (Petoskey). See West Mitchell Street bridge
US-41 Bridge (Houghton County). See Houghton-Hancock Bridge

U. S. Army Board of Inquiry, 148
U. S. Army Corps of Engineers, 93, 148, 160
U. S. Bureau of Public Roads, 38
U. S. Steel and Culvert Company (Bay City, Mich.), 92
U. S. Steel Corporation, 31, 111, 165
United States Supreme Court, 31
Upton Road bridge (Clinton County), 68, **68–69**

Vacationland, 161
Valley Drive, 91
Van Buren County, 90
Van Wagoner, Murray D., 35, **35**
Vanderbilt, Commodore Cornelius, 160
Variety Ironworks (Cleveland, Ohio), 73, 180
Vermontville, 77
Verne, 84

Wabash Bridge Company (Wabash, Ill.), 84, 181
Waddell, J. A. L., 1, 26, 47; *Bridge Engineering,* 19; *The Designing of Ordinary Highway Bridges,* 25, 47
Walker, J. N., 57
Walker, Joseph H., 24
Warren, James, 62
Warren Truss, 62, 77–78, **78**, 84–85
Washington Avenue bridge (Lansing), **112**
Washtenaw County, 73, 75
Wayne County, 12, 13, 80, 94, 100, 109, 121, 123, 145
"Weathering" steel, 145
Welch Road bridge (Ionia County), 82
West Jefferson Avenue bridge (Wayne County), 100
West Main Street (Eagle River Road) bridge (Keweenaw County), 84
West Michigan Avenue bridge (Calhoun County), 117
West Mitchell Street (US-31) bridge (Petoskey), 133, **134–35**
West Verne Road bridge (Saginaw County), 84
Wheaton Bridge Company (Chicago, Ill.), 181
White Creek, 90
Whitefish River, 84
Whitehead & Kales (River Rouge, Mich.), 181
White's Bridge (Ellsworth), **53**
White's Bridge (Ionia County), 11, 57, **57**
Whitney Brothers, Contractors, 133
Williams, Governor G. Mennen ("Soapy"), 161, 165
Wisconsin Bridge & Iron Company (Milwaukee, Wis.), 86, 100, 152, 181
Wolf Creek, 91
Woodfill, William Stewart, 160
Woodruff, Glenn B., 111, 161, 165
Wrought Iron Bridge Company (Canton, Ohio), 31, 48, 64, 73, 75, 181
Wynkoop & McGormley, Agents for Massillon Bridge Company, 68, 181

Ypsilanti, 32

Zilwaukee Bridge, 166–68, **166–67**
Zilwaukee drawbridge, 166

TITLES IN THE GREAT LAKES BOOKS SERIES

Freshwater Fury: Yarns and Reminiscences of the Greatest Storm in Inland Navigation, by Frank Barcus, 1986 (reprint)

Call It North Country: The Story of Upper Michigan, by John Bartlow Martin, 1986 (reprint)

The Land of the Crooked Tree, by U. P. Hedrick, 1986 (reprint)

Michigan Place Names, by Walter Romig, 1986 (reprint)

Luke Karamazov, by Conrad Hilberry, 1987

The Late, Great Lakes: An Environmental History, by William Ashworth, 1987 (reprint)

Great Pages of Michigan History from the Detroit Free Press, 1987

Waiting for the Morning Train: An American Boyhood, by Bruce Catton, 1987 (reprint)

Michigan Voices: Our State's History in the Words of the People Who Lived it, compiled and edited by Joe Grimm, 1987

Danny and the Boys, Being Some Legends of Hungry Hollow, by Robert Traver, 1987 (reprint)

Hanging On, or How to Get through a Depression and Enjoy Life, by Edmund G. Love, 1987 (reprint)

The Situation in Flushing, by Edmund G. Love, 1987 (reprint)

A Small Bequest, by Edmund G. Love, 1987 (reprint)

The Saginaw Paul Bunyan, by James Stevens, 1987 (reprint)

The Ambassador Bridge: A Monument to Progress, by Philip P. Mason, 1988

Let the Drum Beat: A History of the Detroit Light Guard, by Stanley D. Solvick, 1988

An Afternoon in Waterloo Park, by Gerald Dumas, 1988 (reprint)

Contemporary Michigan Poetry: Poems from the Third Coast, edited by Michael Delp, Conrad Hilberry, and Herbert Scott, 1988

Over the Graves of Horses, by Michael Delp, 1988

Wolf in Sheep's Clothing: The Search for a Child Killer, by Tommy McIntyre, 1988

Copper-Toed Boots, by Marguerite de Angeli, 1989 (reprint)

Detroit Images: Photographs of the Renaissance City, edited by John J. Bukowczyk and Douglas Aikenhead, with Peter Slavcheff, 1989

Hangdog Reeef: Poems Sailing the Great Lakes, by Stephen Tudor, 1989

Detroit: City of Race and Class Violence, revised edition, by B. J. Widick, 1989

Deep Woods Frontier: A History of Logging in Northern Michigan, by Theodore J. Karamanski, 1989

Orvie, The Dictator of Dearborn, by David L. Good, 1989

Seasons of Grace: A History of the Catholic Archdiocese of Detroit, by Leslie Woodcock Tentler, 1990

The Pottery of John Foster: From and Meaning, by Gordon and Elizabeth Orear, 1990

The Diary of Bishop Frederic Baraga: First Bishop of Marquette, Michigan, edited by Regis M. Walling and Rev. N. Daniel Rupp, 1990

Walnut Pickles and Watermelon Cake: A Century of Michigan Cooking, by Larry B. Massie and Priscilla Massie, 1990

The Making of Michigan, 1820–1860: A Pioneer Anthology, edited by Justin L. Kestenbaum, 1990

America's Favorite Homes: A Guide to Popular Early Twentieth-Century Homes, by Robert Schweitzer and Michael W. R. Davis, 1990

Beyond the Model T: The Other Ventures of Henry Ford, by Ford R. Bryan, 1990

Life after the Line, by Josie Kearns, 1990

Michigan Lumbertowns: Lumbermen and Laborers in Saginaw, Bay City, and Muskegon, 1870–1905, by Jeremy W. Kilar, 1990

Detroit Kids Catalog: The Hometown Tourist, by Ellyce Field, 1990

Waiting for the News, by Leo Litwak, 1990 (reprint)

Detroit Perspectives, edited by Wilma Wood Henrickson, 1991

Life on the Great Lakes: A Wheelsman's Story, by Fred W. Dutton, edited by William Donohue Ellis, 1991

Copper Country Journal: The Diary of Schoolmaster Henry Hobart, 1863-1864, by Henry Hobart, edited by Philip P. Mason, 1991

John Jacob Astor: Business and Finance in the Early Republic, by John Denis Haeger, 1991

Survival and Regeneration: Detroit's American Indian Community, by Edmund J. Danziger, Jr., 1991

Steamboats and Sailors of the Great Lakes, by Mark L. Thompson, 1991

Cobb Would Have Caught It: The Golden Years of Baseball in Detroit, by Richard Bak, 1991

Michigan in Literature, by Clarence Andrews, 1992

Under the Influence of Water: Poems, Essays, and Stories, by Michael Delp, 1992

The Country Kitchen, by Della T. Lutes, 1992 (reprint)

The Making of a Mining District: Keweenaw Native Copper 1500–1870, by David J. Krause, 1992

Kids Catalog of Michigan Adventures, by Ellyce Field, 1993

Henry's Lieutenants, by Ford R. Bryan, 1993

Historic Highway Bridges of Michigan, by Charles K. Hyde, 1993